Lessons Learned
Along The Way

To John

Lessons Learned Along The Way

GUIDANCE FOR HOW TO LIVE AND LEAD AS DISCIPLES OF JESUS

Rev. John B Hill Jr

ISBN: 1519350511
ISBN 13: 9781519350510

Lessons Learned Along The Way is dedicated to my wife, Terri, my partner in life and ministry, to my clergy friends, Jim Harnish, Dan Johnson, David Dodge, Wayne Curry, Cliff Melvin, Bob Bushong, Gary Spencer, Tim Smiley, Rob Parsons and Jeff Stiggins, and to the staff and leaders of Suntree United Methodist Church, all of whom helped me develop the ideas that make up this book.

Table of Contents

Introduction · ix

Chapter 1   It's Never About What It's About · · · · · · · · · · · ·1
Chapter 2   All Life Is Junior High· · · · · · · · · · · · · · · · ·8
Chapter 3   You Have to Make Bones· · · · · · · · · · · · · · · 14
Chapter 4   Above All Else, Know Thyself · · · · · · · · · · · · 19
Chapter 5   It's Your Call ·25
Chapter 6   You Are More Than What You Do· · · · · · · · · ·32
Chapter 7   You Don't Have to Swing at Every Pitch · · · · ·38
Chapter 8   How You Practice Is How You Will Play · · · · ·44
Chapter 9   Perception Is Not Reality; Reality Is Reality · ·51
Chapter 10 Reading Really Is Fundamental· · · · · · · · · · · ·60
Chapter 11 You Are What You Believe · · · · · · · · · · · · · ·70
Chapter 12 You Put Your Whole Self In · · · · · · · · · · · · ·77

Bibliography ·87

Introduction

It was my first Sunday at my new church appointment in Jacksonville, Florida, and I was in the back of the sanctuary shaking hands and greeting the people of my new congregation, when Mark walked up to me and asked, "Have you ever been backpacking?" No "hello, nice to meet you; good sermon," just an abrupt "have you ever been backpacking?" I had no idea where this conversation was going, so I responded with a cautious and curious, "Noooo…" I was soon to discover that backpacking was the passion of Mark's life, and the only way he would be able to accept me as his pastor was if I went backpacking with him.

Over the next several months, Mark did his best to convince me why I should go backpacking with him. He explained how he had hiked the entire Appalachian Trail several years earlier. He soon convinced me of his experience and his ability to keep me safe on the trail. He showed me a map of the trail in North Carolina that we would hike, and he assured me that it would be an easy ten-day walk through the woods. I finally agreed to go, and we set the date. As I look back, it was his personal experience that was the biggest factor in my decision to go. He knew what he was doing, and he was more than willing to share that experience with me. He taught me how to keep my pack as light as possible by filling it with only the things I would really need. He shared with me what food to take along and how to make meals an enjoyable part of the hike. He taught me how to find clean water, how to read a trail map, and how to protect myself from the bears that tend to visit during the night.

Bears are the greatest threat on the trail. They come into campsites at night looking for food. So you have to make sure that all the dishes are washed, the food scraps are disposed of, and that all the rest of the food is hung high up in a tree. On one trip, a teenage boy who hiked with us did not wash his dishes after dinner, and he stuffed them in his backpack. During the night we heard a bear come into our campsite, and we listened as it got the boy's backpack and carried it away. We found it the next morning a few hundred yards up the trail. His pack had been ripped open, and his dishes were chewed up and no longer useable. Giving bears what they want is the worst mistake you can make on the trail.

When our ten days were over, I had to confess I had a great time. It had been both a mental and a physical test. I agreed to go with Mark again, and I did so for the next six summers.

One of the life lessons I learned from my backpacking adventures is the importance of experience. There were many times I was thankful that Mark knew what he was doing. Because of his experience, he was able to help us avoid dangers and disasters. On more than one occasion, we got lost on some poorly marked trails, but I was never afraid. I knew everything would be OK because I trusted that Mark would guide us to safety.

I am now closing in on the final stretch of my journey in ministry in The United Methodist Church, and I feel it is time for me to share some of the things I have learned along the way. Over my thirty-five years, I have served a wide variety of churches. I have served two small churches that were joined together because they neither could afford a full time pastor on their own, a rural church that was being consumed by the ever-expanding city of Orlando, a small-town church on the east coast of Florida, a rapidly growing church in the suburbs of Jacksonville, and I was copastor with my wife at a very large church in Melbourne, Florida. I have served a church with no paid staff members, and I have served a church with over fifty paid staff members. Over the course of this journey, I have learned some things that I believe might be helpful to others who are working in churches or those who relate to people in other ways on a regular basis. I also believe that some of the lessons that I have learned from my experience will help you be better prepared for the bears that will come growling into your life as they attempt to make a mess of things and demand that you give them what they want.

As I thought about how I could share these life lessons, I decided to share twelve proverbs or maxims that I believe sum up what I have learned. Miguel de Cervantes said proverbs are "short sentences drawn from long experience" (Heath, *Made to Stick*, 2008, 47). In other words, proverbs speak the truth about what we have experienced in this life. However, proverbs speak a limited truth. Many proverbs are not necessarily true in the strictest sense of the word—for example, "a watched pot never boils" or "an apple a day keeps the doctor away." Those are not factually true statements, but we can all understand the truth that is being communicated. The same can be said for the proverbs I will share with you. They will not be true every time and everywhere, but my experience is that they are often more true than we would like to admit.

In his book *The Four Loves*, C. S. Lewis wrote, "Friendship arises out of mere companionship when two or more of the companions discover that they have in common some insight or interest or even taste which the others do not share and which, til that moment, each believed to be his own unique treasure (or burden). The typical expression of opening friendship would be something like, 'What? You too? I thought I was the only one'" (Lewis 1960, 65).

It is my hope that by sharing some of the lessons I have learned along the way, others will be able to say, "What? You too? I thought I was the only one."

CHAPTER 1

It's Never About What It's About

Don AGREED TO BECOME THE chairperson of the finance committee at one of the churches I served. He seemed to be the ideal
person for the job. He was a retired CPA, and he had run his own
company for many years. Besides that, he was in the Sunday-
school class I taught, and I played golf with him on a regular
basis. But the day his new position became official, everything
changed. He refused to listen to anything that I had to say about
the finances of the church, and he constantly came by the office
to tell me that I was going to lead the church into financial ruin.

One day he came to my office, and he was furious. I had
said something at a meeting with which he did not agree, but
everyone else at the meeting thought it was a good idea. He was
angrier than I had ever seen him—and, as I already mentioned,
I played golf with him. In the midst of him reminding me, over
and over again, that I did not know what I was talking about, he
blurted out, "You are just like my son!" He then went on: "You
go off to school, and you get your degree, and you come back
and you think you know everything! You are just like my son,
and I am leaving this church." He stormed out of my office, and
I never saw him again.

After Don left I called the chairperson of the administrative board, who was a friend of Don's, and I told him what had happened. He was a very gracious and understanding man who told me that he did not think that I had done anything wrong. Then he let me in on part of Don's story. Don's son had gone off to college and earned an MBA. When he returned from college, Don turned over the family business to his son. His son quickly began to make some decisions that Don did not agree with, but Don assumed it would all be for the best. Not quite a year after his son took over the business, he told his dad that Don was no longer needed. He insisted that his dad take early retirement, even though he was many years away from when he wanted to retire. Don did as his son asked. He and his wife moved to Florida, and he brought his anger with him.

When I heard the story, I realized that when Don and I began to have our disagreements over finances, he was projecting the anger he had toward his son onto me. (Coincidently, Don's son was the exact same age that I was at the time.) It was my encounter with Don that taught me an important lesson when it comes to dealing with people: "it's never about what it's about."

What I mean is this: when a person's emotionality escalates beyond the appropriate level for any given situation, there is something else going on. There will be times when people will get upset for the right reasons at the right times and at the right people, and, in those cases, it is about what it is about. However, there will be many other times when people's emotions are way over the top for the situation, and when that happens, you have a choice to make. Will you get sucked into the emotionality of the situation, or will you try to figure out what is really going on?

I believe this kind of discernment was something Jesus applied throughout his ministry. People came to him with a question or a problem, but he knew when the real issue was something deeper and more important. John 2:25 says that Jesus "needed no one to testify about anyone; for he himself knew what was in everyone."

This verse sets up the encounter between Jesus and Nicodemus in chapter 3. Nicodemus comes to Jesus by night, supposedly to talk to him about the signs Jesus was doing, but Jesus responds by saying that no one can see the kingdom of God unless he is born from above. Many times in this chapter, it seems like Jesus and Nicodemus are not having the same conversation, and that is because Jesus is answering Nicodemus's real question. Jesus knows what is really going on in Nicodemus's heart and mind. Most of us would readily confess that we are not Jesus, but I do think it is possible for us to become better able to discern what is really going on with people when we get into times of conflict and disagreement.

Theodore Sturgeon was a science-fiction writer in the 1960s. He wrote several episodes of the original *Star Trek* TV series, and he popularized the saying, "Ask the next question." He once wrote, "Every advance this species has ever made is the result of someone, somewhere, looking at his world, his neighborhood, his neighbor...or himself and asking the next question. Every deadly error this species has committed, every sin against itself and its highest destiny, is the result of not asking the next question, or not listening to those who do ask it" (www.physics.emory.edu/~weeks/misc/question.html).

In the midst of highly emotional and deeply conflicted situations, you may not always be able to ask the person the next question: what is this really about? But you can ask it internally. What is really going on here? Is this person's anger appropriate for this situation? And as you ask yourself those sorts of questions, you will become more open to the clues that the person is dropping.

When Don yelled "you are just like my son," he was letting me know that something else was going on and adding to his anger, but I could not hear it at the time because I was getting caught up in the emotionality of the moment. If I had been able to hear what he was really trying to say, I might have been able to salvage our relationship and enable him to remain in the church.

Years later, a man named Woody came to my office, and he too was very upset with me. Sometime earlier, I had started something called Theology at the Tavern. I invited church members and their non church going friends to meet me at a local bar, and we would discuss a variety of theological and philosophical topics in a nonthreatening environment. Since we met in a bar, people were able to get a drink if they so chose. I typically had a glass of wine while I led the discussion. Woody was very upset by this. I tried to explain my rationale for Theology at the Tavern, but everything I said made the situation worse. He became more and more irate; I became more and more defensive. I then reminded him that Jesus drank wine, and he too was accused of being a drunkard. At that point Woody said, "If I were younger, I would come around that desk and beat you up." I believed him. He then left my office, and I began to wonder what would have happened if I had asked him the next question, rather than reacting to his anger with defensiveness. I failed to be a *nonanxious presence.*

I first encountered the idea of being a nonanxious presence in the book *Generation to Generation*, by Edwin Friedman. Basically, you become a nonanxious presence when you are fully present in the conflicted situation, but you are not swept up into the emotionality of the other person. As a nonanxious presence, you do not become defensive because you are aware that you and your behavior are not really the issue. You do not rise up to the other person's level of anger. And as a nonanxious presence, you usually succeed in accomplishing two things: First, you remain calm enough to ask the next question and to discover the real source of the emotionality. Second, if you refuse to match the other person's emotions, he or she will calm down, too—at least a bit.

If I had been less defensive with Woody, I would have asked him why he was so upset with the idea of people drinking at Theology at the Tavern. And my hunch is that he would have told me a painful story about his personal experience with a loved one whose life was destroyed by alcohol. And maybe I could have helped him let go of some of the anger that he was carrying around inside of him. To this day, I do not know what his story was really about, but I know it was about far more than what he said. "It's never about what it's about."

There have been many times when this proverb has proven to be true and helpful. I was once working with a young minister who was having a problem with procrastination. He seemed almost incapable of getting things done on time. He shared with me that he had tried a wide variety of calendars, and he had read several books on time management. After I listened to all he had tried to do in order to solve his problem, I said to him, "I do not think you have a time-management problem." He gave me a rather confused look. I then asked him, "What is it that you are afraid of that is keeping you from doing the things that you are supposed to do?"

It took us a while to figure it out, but his fear was a fear of success. He was so unsure of himself, in large part due to the negativity of his family of origin, that his procrastination was a way to sabotage his ministry. If he continued to be unreliable, then people would not ask him to do more, and he would not have to show people how inadequate he really was. When we discovered what his procrastination was really about, we then could work to overcome it.

Another time, my wife, Terri, met with a woman who was very upset that we misspelled her niece's name in the bulletin. The woman had given flowers in memory of her niece, who had died a year earlier. Terri apologized, but the woman became more and more upset. Her anger was now beyond the level that was appropriate for the situation. Terri realized that it was about something else. Terri asked her to tell her about her niece. The woman described her, and she went on to describe the violent way her niece had been assaulted and then murdered. After she told her niece's tragic story, she took a deep breath and shared that this was the first time she had been able to tell anyone that story. She had been keeping it bottled up inside, and it felt so good to let it out. The greatest source of her anger was not the misspelling of the young woman's name but the tragic way she died. If Terri had stayed focused on the misspelling, she would have missed the opportunity for this woman to take a step toward her own healing and recovery. "It's never about what it's about."

Henry David Thoreau once said, "There are a thousand hacking away at the branches of evil to one who is striking at the root" (*Walden* 1960, 56).

Many times people will come to you, and they will be overly angry, overly worried, overly impatient, or overly afraid. It will be easy for you to get caught up in their level of emotionality, and you will spend all your time hacking away at the branches. But if you seek to become a nonanxious presence so that you can ask the next question, then you will be on your way to discovering what it is really about. And you will be better able to care for and lead those to whom you relate.

CHAPTER 2

All Life Is Junior High

I CAN STILL REMEMBER THE moment I began to accept the truth that all life is a continuation of junior high school. I was taking a group of older adults to a presentation of the passion play in Lake Wales, Florida. As everyone was getting into the church van, I overheard a rather heated conversation that got my attention. Two men were arguing about which one of them was going to ride in the front seat with me. The conversation became more and more intense until one of the men said, "If I cannot ride in the seat next to John, I'm not going to go." I just shook my head in disbelief. What made all this even more unbelievable was that both of the men involved in this argument were retired United Methodist ministers.

The more I thought about that event, the more it reminded me of arguments between my own children. At that time my two daughters were in junior high school, and those two grown men sounded just like my daughters. I then came to understand that many of the conflicts we have with one another feel like the same conflicts that we struggle with in our early teenage years. We want to be in the popular group. We wonder why people don't like us. We struggle to fit in. We question our abilities. We wonder if we will ever be loved. "All life is junior high."

When I first started to share this idea with others, their initial response was that I was being too cynical. One person said the only reason I believed it was because I was stuck in junior high school. But as I explained my thoughts, the more my friends and staff members began to think that maybe I was on to something. They began to think of times in their own lives when it seemed like they were reliving those traumatic teenage years. Now, again, does this mean that all people always act like they are still in junior high school? No, but this proverb often holds true.

A woman once came to me and told me that she had heard of a group of people in the church that was upset with me. They were upset because we had many new people who were attending the church, and they thought that I liked the new people more than I liked them. I assured her that was not the case, and she went back to tell her friends that I still liked them. "All life is junior high."

There are many ways to understand the story of Adam and Eve in the book of Genesis. One of the ways that the story makes sense to me is that Adam and Eve metaphorically represent the developmental stages that are common to us all. The story begins with them in the garden where their Creator and Father, God, takes care of all their needs. They are like little children. They are naked and unafraid. But then comes the time when they seek to find their own way. They rebel against the rules, and they become aware that they are no longer children. They now see that they are naked. They have to move on and become grown-ups. They have to work "by the sweat of their brows," and they have to endure the pain of having their own children.

I believe an argument can be made that Adam and Eve's fall came at the stage of life we often equate with junior high school: the time when we hit puberty and we become much more aware of our bodies and the time when many of us start to rebel against the rules and the wishes of our parents. We might even be able to say that the fall results in a human condition of being stuck in that stage of life where we selfishly seek to get what we want when we want it. One aspect of our fallen nature is to be stuck in junior high school.

The acceptance of that idea is liberating. It has helped me to have more realistic expectations of the people with whom I interact. I am not surprised or shocked when people behave in selfish and self-centered ways. It is also liberating because it tells me that all of us struggle with our share of insecurities. I am not the only one who wonders why I don't seem to fit in, or who struggles with why I am not accepted.

Junior high is also a time of transition. It is a time of change. It is the time when we begin to make the change from childhood to young adulthood. Our bodies change. We begin to make our own decisions, which often run counter to our parents' rules. One of the ways that life is like junior high is we are always in transition. We are always growing and changing. We are always trying to understand who we are and what we are to do. And times of change are always difficult and filled with opportunities for conflict.

In the story of Adam and Eve, Eve sinned when she reached out for the fruit of the tree that would make her like God. She disobeyed God's only rule; however, she did it for a laudable reason. She wanted to become like God. She wanted to know the difference between good and evil. The problem was that she was not ready for such knowledge. She overreached and took what was not hers to take. One of the problems of our early teenage years is that we often want to do things for which we are not yet ready. We try to grow up too soon. As adults much of our sinfulness is the result of disobeying rules, but much of our pain comes from trying to be something we are not. We overreach and we fall. We then question our abilities. Our insecurities become highlighted. We feel like we are in junior high school all over again.

One of the things that I mean when I say that all life is junior high is that we never do outgrow our struggle with many of the insecurities we had as teenagers. I think it is helpful to accept that about one another and about ourselves.

We are not only stuck in junior high because of our inner struggles but also because of some interpersonal behaviors. One of the behaviors that typifies junior high school is triangulation. In *Generation to Generation*, Edwin Friedman defined an emotional triangle in this way: "An emotional triangle is formed by any three persons or issues...The basic law of emotional triangles is that when any two parts of a system become uncomfortable with one another, they will 'triangle in' or focus on a third person or issue, as a way of stabilizing their own relationship with one another" (Friedman 1985, 5). Junior high schoolers are masters at triangulation. When disagreements take place between two friends, another friend is asked to try to resolve the conflict. "Are you still angry with Jan? Do you like Bill?"

Emotional triangles may typify junior-high behavior, but in adulthood they are a sign of a lack of maturity and dysfunction. Yet, we engage in them far more often then we realize. You create a triangle anytime you refuse to address a person or an issue yourself and instead send someone to relay a message for you. This often happens in marriages when the husband and the wife are in conflict and use one of the children to send messages to one another. It happens in our workplaces and in our churches, whenever we try to resolve conflicts and disputes through indirect channels, rather than facing the person we are in conflict with or the issue we want to avoid.

At one of the churches where my wife and I served, we created a staff behavioral covenant that basically said that if any of us had a problem with another staff member, we would first go to that person in order to work it out. One of the key staff members said, "That is impossible for me to do. I have to talk to my friends about it first." She was a master of getting her friends to take her messages to others so that she could appear to be above the fray and have everyone think highly of her.

There are really only two choices you have when you find yourself in an emotional triangle: you can cooperate with this unhealthy behavior, or you can refuse to participate and insist that the conflict or the problem gets resolved in an honest and open way. Jesus said, "If another…sins against you, go and point out the fault when the two of you are alone. If…[he or she] listens to you, you have regained that one" (Matthew 18:15).

Triangles and junior-high-school beliefs and behaviors may go together, but Jesus teaches us how to move beyond them. Jesus tells us to go directly to those with whom we are in conflict. Jesus tells us that we can move beyond the selfish and self-centered lives in which we seem stuck. It is through his grace that he offers to us that which we cannot, or must not, reach out and obtain on our own. He offers us the possibility to become like him...to become like God...to know the difference between good and evil. And it is through his grace that we can come to accept ourselves for who we are as we seek to become the sort of people that God created us to be.

This can happen because God's grace tells us that God loves us and that he accepts us as we are. We do not need to prove ourselves to God in order for him to love us. He understands that we are all stuck in destructive and dysfunctional behaviors, and it is his love that reaches out to us and shows us there is a better way to live.

CHAPTER 3

You Have to Make Bones

§

WHEN I FIRST STARTED MY ministry journey, a wide variety of people gave me the same piece of advice. I was told that when I went to a new church, I shouldn't make any changes for at least a year. This advice came from well-meaning clergy leaders and lay leaders—people who all had a vested interest in maintaining the status quo. There is a great deal of wisdom in this advice, and I followed it for the first fifteen years of my ministry. For the most part, it worked out well for me. My appointments during those years were small, loving churches where I felt loved and welcomed into their communities.   After fifteen years and three appointments, I was sent to a new church. I left a church that had three part-time employees and went to a church with a staff of fifteen. I went from a church that was extremely healthy and happy to one that was deeply divided because of the previous pastor's unethical behavior. As I prepared for ministry in this new situation, I did so with the mantra, "Don't make any changes for at least a year."

I abandoned that advice a month later. I went to my first church-council meeting, which was more like a barroom brawl than a board meeting. People yelled at each other and called each other names, and I sat there in shock. The next morning,

I asked people about what had taken place, and I was told that was a typical church-council meeting. I was told that there had once been a fistfight after an especially heated meeting. They told me that was just how they did things at that church.

The following month I went to my second church-council meeting, and I was ready to make a change. We were just a few minutes into the meeting when one of the lay leaders began to question the integrity of a staff member who was giving a report. The lay leader ended his criticism by saying, "You are just a liar." I walked to the front of the room, and I said, "As long as I am the pastor of this church, this behavior is going to change. There will be no more yelling and no more name-calling. We are going to treat one another with respect." I drew a line in the sand. And I did so in a way that it was clear that I passionately believed what I said.

After the meeting, several individuals thanked me for what I had said. But not everyone was happy with me. I soon discovered that two women were passing around a petition to have me moved. The petition never did get much support, so the two of them gave up—at least for a while.

It was about at this same time that I first heard the expression, "You have to make bones." To "make bones" means that you have to kill someone in order to become a part of some criminal gang. In W. E. B. Griffin's novel *The Assassin*, he explains it this way: "In order to be a real mobster, you have to kill somebody...They call it 'making your bones.'" After hearing this, I began to wonder if that isn't also what we need to do when we enter into a new church or new business setting. I am not suggesting that we literally kill someone. What I mean is that I now believe that you should not passively sit back and make no changes over your first year. Instead, I believe that you should look for strategic changes you can make that will communicate to people what is really important to you.

The people you are leading want to know what you are passionate about. They want to know if there is anything that you would "kill" for. I believe the people you lead want you to "make bones" as they decide whether or not they will accept you into their system. And if you wait for "at least a year" to let them know what is really important to you, it will be too late. By making bones you gain respect and credibility and you preserve your ability to lead. You have to make bones.

Ten years later, I was appointed to a new church, as the co-pastor with my wife. It was a very large church with over one thousand in attendance on Sunday morning. After we got there, we had a meeting with the staff leaders, and we asked them to share with us one or two words that they felt best described the church. We were shocked by the responses: upper class, affluent, country club, white. The vast majority of the staff said these things with a sense of pride. Terri and I worked to change this attitude, which was not just held by staff members but was also held by many of the lay leaders of the church. We made little progress.

During those first few months at the church, when I would tell people in the community that I was one of the ministers at the local United Methodist church, their usual response was, "Oh, that's the big church down the road." We were the big, wealthy, mostly white, country-club church.

The next summer, Florida was overwhelmed by three hurricanes—one of which did a lot of damage to our community. Most of the houses in our area lost power for over a week, but not our facility. We had a decision to make. How were we going to respond to this disaster? Were we going to focus our energy on making repairs to our church, since we did sustain some structural damage, or would we focus on the needs of the people around us? Most of the staff wanted to turn inward and take care of our buildings and themselves. Terri and I decided that we were going to reach out to the community. We served free meals. We gave away free ice. We opened up the church and invited people to come in and sit in the air-conditioning and escape the heat and the heartache for a while.

After things got back to normal, a woman in the church came to me and said, "What you did in response to the hurricane has defined your ministry here." We made bones.

A few days later, I was in the grocery store, and I got into a conversation with the cashier. I told her that I was one of the ministers at the local United Methodist church, and she said, "Oh, you mean the church that helps people." We were still the big church, but that was no longer what defined us.

We had let people know that we passionately believed that we could no longer be the country-club church that ignored the needs of the people around us. We let them know that we were willing to kill, or die, for that. We made bones.

Today, the vision of that church is "…to be followers of Jesus who love God, love each other, and love our neighbors in extraordinary ways." It took us five difficult years to get there, but I do not think we would have ever gotten there if we had not made bones within that first year.

Jesus said, "For those who want to save their life will lose it, and those who lose their life for my sake will find it" (Matthew 16:25). I believe that Jesus was talking to us about our basic human desire to maintain the status quo as we try to hold onto what we have. This principle is true for individuals and institutions. It is true for churches and companies. We all resist change and try to keep things the way they are. I believe it is out of that desire that we hear the advice, "Don't change anything for at least a year." If you follow that advice, then you will probably never make any significant change to the existing system, because you will have become a part of that system.

When you try to save your life by holding onto what you already have, you lose the opportunity to discover a better way. But if you will take a risk and let go of what you have and how you have always done it, then all sorts of new—and possibly better—ways of leading and living will be opened to you. Jesus calls it "dying to self."

Martin Luther King Jr. said, "If you haven't found something worth dying for, you aren't fit to be living." What are you willing to die for? What will you stand up for, no matter what the cost? To join with a criminal gang, you have to make bones by killing someone else. To join with Jesus and allow him to lead you as you lead others, you have to make bones by finding those things for which you would die.

CHAPTER 4

Above All Else, Know Thyself

§

SEVERAL YEARS AGO, I READ an article that said if you want to get to know someone quickly, ask the person to name his or her five favorite movies of all time. The article suggested that our favorite movies reveal a lot about who we are and how we see the world around us. My top four are *Monty Python and the Holy Grail, Butch Cassidy and the Sundance Kid, Three Days of the Condor,* and *Goldfinger.* I struggle to choose a fifth favorite. One of the movies that most often makes it into fifth place is *Bull Durham.*

Bull Durham is about the romance between an aging, minor-league baseball catcher—Crash Davis (Kevin Costner)—and a baseball groupie and community-college teacher—Annie Savoy (Susan Sarandon). In the movie Annie Savoy often tries to make deeply philosophical statements about life and baseball. One of the best is "the world is made for people who aren't cursed with self-awareness."

If it is true that the world is populated by people who behave like they are in junior high school, then it follows that most of us are also cursed with a lack of self-awareness. Self-awareness is not an attribute we normally associate with junior high school. It would also follow that one of the most helpful things you can do in order to be set free from the curse of junior high is to grow in your self-awareness. "Above all else, know thyself."

The statement "know thyself" is often attributed to Socrates, but when Plato quotes him, it is assumed that Socrates is referring to a long-standing philosophical truth. The words *know thyself* appear in the courtyard of the Temple of Apollo at Delphi. Even though this statement did not originate with Socrates, it had a major impact upon his philosophy. His belief that we are to know ourselves was a big part of the reason he continually asked questions that would help people come to a greater level of self-awareness. After Socrates was sentenced to death, by those who were upset with his unrelenting questions, he said, "The unexamined life is not worth living" (*Great Dialogues of Plato*, 1956, 443).

A life that is worth living is one in which you examine your thoughts, your feelings, and your motives so you can know yourself. Why is it that I think the way I do? Why do I let certain things bother me so much? Why do I do the things I do? Those are the sorts of questions that lead us to greater self-awareness.

I believe Jesus was inviting us into this process of self-examination when he said that we have to first take the log out of our own eye before we try to take the speck out of our neighbor's eye. (See Matthew 7:3–5.) As is so often the case, Jesus is using the humor of hyperbole to get our attention and to make his point. He is trying to tell us that before we can help others, we have to examine our own lives. We have to look within ourselves so that we can begin to understand our motivations, our prejudices, and our intentions if we want to help others deal with theirs.

I believe that the difficult process of "taking the log out of your own eye" is meant to make us more sensitive and caring as we help to "take the speck out of our neighbor's eye." However, many people read this passage and assume that it is the pathway to becoming judgmental. They assume that if they acknowledge that they are sinners who are forgiven by God, then they can run around and point out everyone else's sin. I do not believe that Jesus is telling us what we have to do in order to become able to judge other people. Rather, I believe that the process of genuine self-examination will cause us to become less judgmental and more compassionate and understanding. We understand how painful it is to take an honest look at who we are and why we do what we do. It is painful, but it is also eye-opening.

I once met with a pastor who was struggling in his ministry. The people in the church were continually criticizing him because of the poor decisions he was making. As I listened to him tell me about some of those decisions, which really were not wise, I said something about his need for greater self-awareness. He looked at me and asked, "What do you mean by 'self-awareness'?"

He really had no clue what it meant to be self-aware. And that was the source of many, if not all, of his difficulties as a pastor. He did things without ever reflecting on why he was doing them. He never asked why he was getting angry. He never asked why he was ignoring the advice of well-meaning church leaders. He never asked the next question. He was reacting without reflecting. In the book *Leadership and Self-Deception*, this pastor's lack of self-awareness would be called "self-deception." Self-deception is refusing to see the log in your own eye. It is refusing, or being afraid, to ask yourself the question "why?" Why did I do that? It was Benjamin Franklin who said, "Who has deceived thee so often as thyself?"

"Above all else, know thyself." By self-awareness I mean that you need to seek to understand yourself. You need to reflect on your past experiences and try to see how they have worked together to make you who you are. Why does my parents' excessive criticism cause me to procrastinate today? Why do I continue to allow the rejection and pain of junior high school to shape my reactions to life? Why am I so filled with fear? Why am I so negative? Why do I spend so much of my time and energy trying to convince people that I am a good person? Why is it so hard for me to admit my faults? Why do I turn everything into a competition? Questions like these, and many others, can help us to begin to enter into the process of self-awareness.

Some people enter into the process of self-awareness naturally and easily. Others need the help of counselors and guides. When I was in seminary, I took one semester of clinical pastoral education (CPE). CPE involved working as a chaplain in a clinical environment, discussing that work in a group-therapy setting, and meeting with an advisor. The group therapy and the advisor served to push us to get more in touch with our feelings and the feelings of others. I remember one session with my advisor when I told her that I was a fairly calm and laid-back guy. As I said this, I drew a straight line in the air with my hand. My advisor smiled and said, "You do know what a flat line like that means in a hospital, don't you?" She was helping me to see that I was trying to avoid some of my deeper feelings, which, in turn, was keeping me from being fully alive. I needed her help in order to see these things about myself.

I also believe that trusted friends who ask us the tough and probing questions that we often choose to ignore can be a great help in the process of self-awareness. I have friends—clergy and lay—and a spouse who care enough about me to push me to ask the questions that I often try to avoid. When we avoid those difficult and probing questions, we tend to stay on a very superficial level of life. Jesus says, "I came that they [you and me] may have life and have it abundantly" (John 10:10). Jesus came so that you can do more than live life on the surface. He came so that he could help to guide you into a deeper understanding of who you are and who you can become.

Self-awareness is not just the process of asking why we think and feel and do the things we do; it is also coming to accept the limit of our own knowledge. Socrates once said, "True knowledge is found when we acknowledge our ignorance." In Romans 7:15, the Apostle Paul says, "I do not understand my own actions. For I do not do what I want, but I do the very thing I hate." Part of coming to know yourself is knowing what you do not know. People often ask me if I believe in absolute truth. My answer is, "Yes, I believe in absolute truth. The problem is that I cannot know it with my limited mind." To become self-aware is to admit what you do not, and cannot, know.

In the remake of the movie *Casino Royale*, M—the head of MI6—says to James Bond, "Arrogance and self-awareness seldom go hand in hand." If you want to grow in your self-awareness, you must acknowledge your limits—especially the limits of what you know and what you understand. Again, I think that is also a part of what Jesus was saying with the whole log-in-the-eye thing. We can only really help someone with the speck in his or her eye when we accept that we cannot fully understand why it is there. And that is why we cannot arrogantly judge others for the specks in their eyes. We will never have enough information to judge anyone. Only God knows all about you and me, so only God is able to judge.

It is fair to ask at this point, "What is the difference in being judgmental and pointing out the speck in my neighbor's eye?" For me, it again comes down to self-awareness. Before I can point out the speck in my neighbor's eye, I have to be clear about why I am doing it. If I am pointing out the speck in his or her eye so that I can make that person feel guilt or shame or so that I can feel better about myself, then that is being judgmental, and I still have to work on that log in my eye. But if I want to help my neighbor with some problem because I genuinely care for him or her, then I am able to do so without judgment. In my understanding, we are judgmental when we try to put someone down. We are acting out of care and compassion when we try to help people up. Being judgmental arises out of arrogance. Care and compassion arise out of self-awareness.

If Socrates is right, and the unexamined life is not worth living, then it is by knowing ourselves and growing in our self-awareness that we find the life that is worth living. As we grow in our self-awareness, we can let go of our unhealthy need to impress others and simply enjoy the moments we have with family and friends. We can overcome the fear of our deep feelings, and we can then be with a loved one in a time of overwhelming tragedy. We can learn to love ourselves, and that is when we can truly love our neighbors, who will always come with specks in their eyes.

"Above all else, know thyself."

CHAPTER 5

It's Your Call

§

EVERY MINISTER I HAVE EVER known has wanted to quit and do something else. The reasons we want to quit vary from person to person, but the reasons seem to fall into similar categories.

Some ministers want to quit because they are tired of dealing with the childish behavior of many of the people in their churches. "All life is junior high."

Others want to quit because they do not feel like they can meet the expectations of the people around them, whether they are lay people or denominational leaders.

There are those who want to quit so that they can lead a more sane life. People in this category usually talk about getting a nine-to-five job, where they can walk away from problems at the end of the day.

Still others want to quit because they are frustrated by the lack of accomplishment or progress in their churches. People in this category often want to find a job where they can actually see that they have made some measurable difference. I cannot remember a single time when I have heard a minister say that he or she wanted to quit in order to make more money.

The reality is that most ministers want to quit because they are frustrated with the church. They are frustrated with the lack of progress. They are frustrated because they remember that they were called to lead and serve churches, and these churches often resist their leadership. They remember their calling, and that is why they do not quit, in spite of the regular urge. I am convinced that it is the conviction that we have been called by God that enables and empowers us to keep doing the challenging task of ministry. The reverse is also true; you will not be able to complete the journey of ministry without a clear sense that God has called you to that role. "It's your call."

My call to ministry started when my family moved to Bismarck, North Dakota. I was twelve years old, and my family had not gone to church for many years. When we got to Bismarck, my parents decided that they needed to return to church so their children could get some religious education. We started attending the local United Methodist church because my parents were told that "the Methodist church did not have any rules," and they wanted to avoid the rule-laden church of their childhood. Dave Knecht was the pastor of the church, and I was immediately drawn to him. He always seemed happy. He seemed to enjoy what he was doing. It also seemed like what he was doing at the church was not that hard—little did I know then. I decided that I wanted to be like Rev. Dave when I grew up.

Over the next several years, I got more and more involved in the church. Rev. Dave encouraged me to participate in the Sunday morning services. I continued to want to be like Rev. Dave when I grew up. Then came the summer of 1973. Our youth group went on a mission trip to Greenville, Mississippi, so that we could work in the Delta Mission. We helped with voter registration in the African

American community, we helped to organize transportation for the upcoming elections, and we worked on rebuilding an abandoned community center. At the end of our time there, we had a big celebration picnic. During the picnic, I walked to the edge of the park and sat down under a shade tree, and I watched a group of white kids from North Dakota talking and eating and laughing and playing with impoverished African American kids from Mississippi. I was filled with a sense of joy. It was then that I heard "the still, small voice" of God (1 Kings 19:12 KJV) say to me, "This is what I want you to spend your life doing."

I heard God calling me to spend my life serving the church, which has the message and the ability to change the world. Even as I retell that story, forty-three years later, I am filled with emotion. It is because of that call that I go to work the morning after an awful church meeting. It is because of that call that I go to work, even though I know I will have to deal with upset staff members. It is because of that call that I have never followed through with my desire to quit. For me, it all goes back to the call. If you have a clear sense of a call from God, you can make it through this journey of ministry. Without it, you should not even start.

In his book *The Faith of the Christian Church*, Tyron Inbody says this about the call to ministry: "This calling consists, first, of the call to be a Christian, the call to hear the Word of God, the call to discipleship...It consists, second, of an inner persuasion that God has a special purpose for one's life and that one is summoned, even commanded, by God to obey that call. It includes, third, a providential call, which is sometimes referred to as 'gifts and graces' for specialized ministry...A call includes, finally, an ecclesiastical call, an invitation extended by the church...to engage in the work of representative ministry" (Inbody 2005, 269).

Up to this point, I have been focusing on the second part of the call, which is the call to ordained ministry, but I think it is important to remember that all Christians have a call upon their lives. As Christians we have the call to be disciples of Jesus in all areas of our lives. We all have a vocation.

Vocation comes from the Latin word for a call or a summons. It was originally used to let all Christians know that they were called to join in the work of the church for the transformation of the world. Later it was expanded to mean that the work you did in order to earn money was also a calling from God. It was understood that God had given you the gifts and talents to do the job to which you were called. So, in the broadest understanding of this word, we all have a call from God to serve God in our daily lives.

I believe that when people discover a way of making a living that uses their God-given gifts and talents, they find joy and contentment in their work, and that keeps them going in the difficult times. I have often heard that Confucius said, "Find a job you love, and you will never work a day in your life." That is one of those proverbs that is not true. If you find a job—a vocation—that you love, there will be days when it doesn't feel like work. But, even when you are doing something that you love, there will be many days when it is just hard work.

All Christians are also called to work in the church. Not all are called to the specialized work of ordained ministry, but all are called to the general work of the church. Once again, if you can work and serve in the church by using the gifts God has given to you, then that work will be a joyful and rewarding experience. One way to discover what your gifts are is to take one of the many spiritual-gifts inventories that are out there. For those of you who do not think you have a God-given gift for the general ministry of the church, know that the Apostle Paul would disagree with you. "Now there are varieties of gifts, but the same Spirit; and there are varieties of service, but the same Lord; and there are varieties of activities, but it is the same God who activates all of them in *everyone*. To *each* is given the manifestation of the Spirit for the common good" (1 Corinthians 12:4–7). All Christians have a vocation, a calling, to serve Jesus through the ministry of the church.

Several years ago, I was at a gathering, and a very prestigious and popular pastor said that all pastors who did not have the spiritual gift of leadership should go home and resign from their churches. I understood what he was trying to say, but I disagreed with him. I think he was trying to say that all clergy are called to lead their churches, and if you are not willing to lead, then you should quit. But you do not have to have the spiritual gift of leadership in order to lead. I have a close friend whose main spiritual gift is hospitality. He has learned how to lead out of his gift of hospitality. Under his leadership, people feel welcomed into the church, and it becomes a safe place for the laity to step up and use their gifts. He may not have the gift of leadership, but he has a style that brings out the best in people. My friend will soon be retiring from many years of fruitful ministry because he felt called by God to use the gifts God had given him.

For some, there will come a time when they feel they are called to a more specific and specialized ministry. When that happens, I believe you have to ask the question, "Can I do what God is calling me to do as a dedicated layperson?" If we take this question seriously, it will have two consequences for the church. One, it will lift up the ministry of the laity. Far too many of the clergy in the church treat the laity as if they are just to be spectators to the ministry that is done by the clergy and the paid staff. There needs to be a renewal of the challenge of the Reformation to acknowledge the "priesthood of all believers." I believe this is vital for the church as we move ahead into the future because more and more young people are going to want to have a hands-on ministry, rather than have everything handed to them.

The second thing this question will do is help us to recognize the uniqueness of the role of clergy people. This may seem to be in contradiction to what I just offered up; however, by *uniqueness* I do not mean superiority. The role of the clergy is not superior to that of the laity; it is just different. We must be clear that clergy and laity are in cooperation as we answer the call of God to serve the church as we seek to transform the world. That is our call.

Having an inner sense of call is vital in the journey of ministry. As I have explained, without that inner sense of call, you will not be able to continue or complete this journey. However, you must also have the external call of the church, and that is true for clergy and laity alike. The church—the local church and the denomination—has an essential role to play. As a lay-person you may feel called to teach in your local church; you may have the spiritual gift of teaching and the ability to teach, but your church has to be in agreement with you before you can teach. The leadership may have valid reasons for why you are not ready to teach in that setting, and you need to respect those reasons.

For those who seek to become ordained, you will have to go through a process by which your local church or your denomination discerns your call. When they affirm your call, it is a joyous experience. When they do not affirm your call, it is a painful experience that usually causes you to become very angry. But, again, they will have their reasons, which you need to accept as part of the process. They may suggest things you need to do in order to better prepare yourself, or they may suggest that you are better suited for a different denomination. I served on such a denominational committee for twelve years, and, in my experience, we always wanted to arrive at a decision that was best for the individual and that was best for the local churches of our denomination. The inner call and the outer call are both important and necessary.

As Christians we are all called to serve God through the work of the church. It is a great calling. "It's your call."

CHAPTER 6

You Are More Than What You Do

THERE ARE TWO TIMES WHEN I am very reluctant to tell people that I am a United Methodist minister: when I am on the golf course and when I am on vacation. The typical pattern when I play golf with someone I do not know is that on about the fourth hole, the person will ask me, "What do you do for a living?" It is usually an uncomfortable moment because, over the course of the first three holes, the person has usually yelled out a few four-letter words, thrown his or her clubs, or told a questionable joke. As soon as I reveal the secret that I am a minister, the other player starts to apologize and ask for forgiveness. This new information so affects my opponent that it messes up the rest of the person's round.

The reason for my reluctance to share what I do for a living when I am on vacation is totally different and much more self-centered. When I go on vacation, I do not want to work. There is a difference between vocation and vacation. When I am on vacation and people discover that I am a minister, they begin to ask me questions about their dead relatives or what they should do about their friend who insists that he is an atheist. When I am on vacation, I want to take a break from offering up advice and dealing with church politics. On one vacation, I came up with the perfect response to the inevitable question, "What do you do for a living?" I told people I worked for my Father. It worked, but I did feel a bit dishonest.

When I am out playing golf or spending time with friends or on vacation with my family, I am comfortable stepping out of the pastoral role for a while. Unfortunately, I do not think that is the case for far too many who are in the ministry.

Several years ago, there was an article in the *New York Times* called "Taking a Break from the Lord's Work." The article shared that members of the clergy have a higher rate of obesity, hypertension, and depression than most other Americans. The writer of this article cited studies that connected the clergy's poor health with the fact that most of us do not take a break from our pastoral lives. In the article, an assistant professor of health research at Duke University is quoted as saying, "These people (clergy) tend to be driven by a sense of duty to God to answer every call for help from anybody, and they are virtually called upon all the time."

The article also said that studies show that members of the clergy have "boundary issues," which is defined as "being too easily overtaken by the urgency of other people's needs."

The conclusion of the article is that members of the clergy are unhealthy—physically and psychologically—because we fail to take time off for time away. That may be true, but I think there is a deeper problem that must be dealt with...one that a good vacation cannot resolve. (Remember, it is never about what it is about.) The problem that clergy, and most other people, fail to deal with is a lack of self-differentiation.

My basic definition of self-differentiation is the state when a person is not dependent on external relationships or circumstances for his or her sense of self-worth. This means that self-differentiated people are not swayed by the expectations of those who try to tell them what they should do or how they should respond to a given situation. That is why it is so difficult for members of the clergy to be self-differentiated; we have a steady stream of people who are very willing to tell us what we should do and how we are to respond. If we want these people to stay in the church and not take their ball and go home, we will play the game by their rules. (Remember, all life is junior high.) The result of this pressure is that ministers often try to make everyone happy and fulfill all the expectations of those in our churches, and we do this because we believe that our sense of worth comes from the approval and acceptance of the people in our churches.

One day, early in my ministry, I was in the garage trying to fix my child's bike when my wife, Terri, came out to see what I was doing. (She probably heard me letting out a few four-letter words of my own.) Since she was there, I said, "I have made a big decision. I am no longer going to look to the church for approval."

When I said that, I was not so much thinking about the people of the local church I was serving at the time; I was thinking about the people in authority over me, like district superintendents and the bishop. For several years I lived with the fantasy that I would get a call from the bishop or my district superintendent just because he or she wanted to tell me what a good job I was doing and that my spiritual overseer was proud of me. I was like a young boy desperately looking for his father's approval, and I was working hard for that approval. And then, one day, I decided to stop seeking the approval of the people around me. I accepted that I was someone who was loved by God and called by God, and that became enough for my sense of self-worth. I wish I could say that I never wavered from that, but self-differentiation is not something you do in a single moment. It is an ongoing process that most of us will struggle with until the day we die.

"You are more than what you do." This proverb is key to understanding how to become a self-differentiated person. You are more than what you do for a living, so you can take a vacation. You are more than what you do for people, so you can say no to what they want or expect. You are more than what you do, because the essence of the message of Jesus Christ is grace. Because of grace we understand that we cannot earn God's love through the things we do. "You are more than what you do."

One of my favorite characters in the Bible is David. He was a faithful, yet flawed, servant of God. One of the more familiar stories from David's life is his battle with Goliath. When David shows up where the Israelites are camped, his oldest brother, Eliab, meets him and says, "What are you doing here? Did you leave the few sheep you have to watch in the wilderness?" (1 Samuel 17:28). In other words he was telling his little brother to go home.

Later in the story, David meets with King Saul, who says, "You can't fight the giant; you are just a boy" (1 Samuel 17:33).

David refused to let his brother or his king tell him what he could do or should do. He was unwilling to accept their expectations. His refusal to wear King Saul's armor was another way to say that he would not go into battle like anyone else; he would do it his way. David was a self-differentiated leader.

Some time later, when David became king of Israel, he danced before the ark of the covenant, and afterward his wife, Michal, let him have it. "How the king of Israel honored himself today, uncovering himself today before the eyes of his servants' maids, as a vulgar fellow might shamelessly uncover himself." In other words, she was saying that he was not doing what a king should do. David was not meeting her expectations. How did David respond? "I danced before the Lord…" He did not dance for her or for her approval. He danced for God. (See 2 Samuel 6:12–23.)

In *Generation to Generation*, Friedman wrote about our need to be self-differentiated in our families and in our churches. He said, "Differentiation means the capacity to be an 'I' while remaining connected" (Friedman 1985, 27).

One of the greatest dangers of becoming self-differentiated is that you can distance yourself from the people you love and are called to serve. As you become more and more able to believe that you do not need other people's approval and acceptance for your sense of self-worth, you can go too far and believe that you are better off without them. You then become distant and withdrawn. And that is not a good place to be. Instead, you need to remain connected to the people around you, while at the same time not allowing them to force you into being something or someone you are not. As a self-differentiated person, the better way to deal with people is to say, "This is who I am, and this is what God is calling me to do; will you go with me?" (Kind of sounds like how Jesus called his disciples.)

As self-differentiated people, we will be able to be a nonanxious presence in times of conflict or disagreement. You are a nonanxious presence when you can remain confident and comfortable in who you are and, at the same time, not allow the emotions of others to control your reaction. A self-differentiated person is more often able to discern when it's not about what it's about. A self-differentiated person can usually see junior-high behavior for what it is and not join in. A self-differentiated person is able to "make bones," even if it will not make everyone happy. A self-differentiated person is able to stay connected to people while remaining true to herself or himself.

CHAPTER 7

You Don't Have to Swing at Every Pitch

§

As a young boy, I played Little League Baseball, and it was one of the things I enjoyed the most about my childhood. However, I do have one memory from a game that I did not enjoy. I was standing in the on-deck circle, waiting to take my turn at bat, when the pitcher hit me in the head with a wild pitch. I was surprised. I was angry. I was embarrassed as people pointed at me and laughed at what had happened. I did not think it was funny at all. When I got into the batter's box, I was determined to get a hit to get back at the pitcher for hitting me in the head. I proceeded to take three big swings at his first three pitches. I swung at a ball in the dirt, a ball way outside, and a ball over my head. If you stop and think about what I did, you have to admit that it was not a wise strategy. Here was a pitcher who was so wild that he missed the plate by ten feet when he hit me in the head, and I was swinging at every pitch he threw me. I struck out. I went back to the dugout without accomplishing my goal. I was more upset and angry than when I went to the plate. It was a miserable experience, but it taught me an important lesson. "You don't have to swing at every pitch."

There will be many times when people want you to make decisions quickly, before you have the information you need. They will want you to take a swing at their pitch. And far too often, you will do just that. We swing at people's pitches because we want to do what they want and make them happy. We swing because their request doesn't seem like that big of a deal. We swing because we don't have the time to find out details. We swing because it feels good to come to someone's rescue. We swing because it gives us the illusion that we are the one in control of the situation. But when someone is trying to get you to make a decision quickly, before you can gather more information, you are not the person who is in control.

I often found myself in this situation when Terri and I were copastors at a church. The staff members she supervised would come to me when she was not in the office and tell me that they had a problem or a need that had to be resolved immediately. They needed me to do something about it because it could not wait until Terri returned. They were making their pitch, and they wanted me to take a swing. And I usually did. Later, when I would tell Terri what I had done, she would give me more of the story. Typically, I would discover that she had already spoken to that staff member and had given the person an answer with which he was not happy or with which she did not agree. So the staff member waited until Terri was gone to see if he or she could get it past me. This did not make these staff members bad people. It was a really good staff. It is just one more reminder that all life is junior high. If Mom says no, I will go see if I can get Dad to say yes. The biggest clue that someone is trying to get you to swing at a pitch that you shouldn't is that they do not want to give you time to think about it. It has to be done right now. It is urgent. There is no time for questions.

In the eighth chapter of the Gospel of John, a group of religious leaders brought a woman, whom they had caught in the act of adultery, to Jesus. They reminded him that the penalty for such an act was to be stoned to death, and they wanted Jesus to make a decision about what should be done with her. They threw a pitch to Jesus, and they wanted him to take a swing. Instead, Jesus squatted down and began to write in the dirt.

Over the years, there have been some wildly creative theories about what Jesus wrote in the dirt. One theory is that he wrote the sins of each of the men who were standing around him with stones in their hands. Another is that he wrote out the words of Deuteronomy 22:22: "If a man is caught lying with the wife of another man, both of them shall die, the man who lay with the woman as well as the woman. So you shall purge the evil from Israel."

I think Jesus wrote in the dirt so he could take charge of the situation. He paused. He doodled in the dirt. And then all the people gathered around him were confused. He was not doing what they wanted. They kept pushing him for an answer. But Jesus took control of the moment and said, "Let anyone among you who is without sin be the first to throw a stone at her." He then went back to doodling in the dirt, and all the men dropped their stones and went to their homes (John 8:1–11).

The religious leaders came with a pitch that they hoped Jesus would take a swing at and miss, but he waited for his pitch, and he hit it out of the park. "You don't have to swing at every pitch."

Think about some of the wild offers that come to us by way of TV commercials. We hear about a deal that is too good to be true, and the announcer says, "You must decide quickly. Quantities are limited. You must call in the next five minutes." When people come to you with a sense of urgency and they want you to make a decision in that moment, you need to slow down and ask yourself if this is really a pitch worth your swing. A major-league baseball player has less than half a second to decide if he is going to swing at a pitch. We have much more time than that...more time than we are usually led to believe.

There will be other times when people will try to get you to swing at their pitch—not because they want to get something past you, but because they want to make you look bad or make it look like you do not know what you are doing. This was the religious leaders' hope when they brought Jesus the woman caught in the act of adultery. If Jesus said to stone her, then he could have been turned over to the Romans because they did not allow the Jewish people to stone their lawbreakers. If he said not to stone her, they would have accused him of breaking their laws. The Jewish leaders wanted Jesus to look bad because they saw him as a threat to their power and their influence. Whenever you are in a power struggle with another person, you need to carefully choose the pitches when you will swing.

I had some disagreements with a woman in one of my churches about how things should be done. She was a powerful force in the church, and she was used to getting her way. When she did not get her way, she began to spread rumors about me that were not true. One of her favorite things to say was that I often lost my temper with her and yelled at her. When I heard what she was saying, I did get angry, and I was tempted to confront her. Fortunately, I realized that is exactly what she wanted. If I expressed my anger with her, then it would help to confirm what she was saying to people. She wanted me to swing at her pitch, but I refused to do so.

At other times, people will try to get you to respond in a certain way because they want to get you on their side of an issue or decision. I once had a man come to my office and volunteer to teach a Sunday-school class. At that time we had a desperate need for another teacher, and he seemed like a good choice. Several weeks later, he appeared before the city council to argue in favor of a highly controversial issue; it was an issue I was opposed to, as were the majority of people in the church. As he argued his case, he repeatedly said that he was a Sunday-school teacher at the church I served. I became guilty by association. A swing and a miss.

Has your spouse ever said something that felt like he or she was just trying to start an argument? Has a child ever made an outrageous statement for no apparent reason? Has your boss ever told you that you had to do something before the end of the day? Have you ever felt like a friend was forcing you to make a decision? In those situations, a pitch is being thrown, and you have to decide what you are going to do. Sometimes you need to swing. Other times, it is best for you to lay off that pitch.

When you decide not to swing at a pitch, you are giving yourself an opportunity to figure out the best way to respond. It is a time when you can become a nonanxious presence who listens but who does not automatically respond to the emotion-ality or the urgency of the other person. It is a time when you can take a step back and ask yourself what is really taking place in this moment. Are there options other than the ones that are being offered? If you swing at this pitch, are you really helping this person, or are you being used in a way that will not be help-ful in the long run? No one can force you to swing at pitches. You are the one who chooses how and when you will respond. "You don't have to swing at every pitch."

I once heard that, when Charles Eliot was president of Harvard University, he said, "This year I'm told that the [base-ball] team did well because our pitcher has a fine curveball. I understand that a curveball is thrown with a deliberate at-tempt to deceive. Surely this is not an ability we should want to foster at Harvard." There will be times when people will intentionally try to deceive you with their request—their pitch. There will be times when they just want to get their way... times when they want to make you look bad...times when they are in a power struggle with you...times when they need to get you on their side. But you do not have to swing at every pitch that comes your way. You can be patient. You can wait. You can ask the next question. You can try to discern what it is really about. And when you get the information you need, then you can swing away.

CHAPTER 8

How You Practice Is How You Will Play

§

WHEN I WAS IN HIGH school, I was on the track team. Our track team had a great reputation because we were the state champions for six straight years, two of which were my sophomore and junior years. As I entered my senior year, it was fully expected that we would win the state meet that year as well.

Very early in the season, we were scheduled to go to an indoor meet that had teams from three different states. Our coach decided that he was only going to take twelve of us to the meet; I was excited to be one of the twelve. A couple of days before the meet, the coach wanted some of us to work on our starts. I did not have to spend much time on my starts because I ran the 440 (this was back when the races were measured in yards and not meters), and the start was not an important part of that event.

We got the starting blocks out, set them according to our preferences, and one of the assistant coaches loaded the starter's pistol. After several practice starts, several of us thought it would be fun to try to anticipate the start, which means we tried to guess when the coach would fire the pistol, instead of waiting to hear it. The danger in doing this is that you might move too soon and have a false start. That is what happened to me. When the head coach saw what was going on, he walked over to us, looked at me, and said, "How you practice is how you will play."

We traveled to the meet, which was a much bigger deal than any of us had imagined. We were just one team among many, not the defending state champions. The time came for the 440. I went to my lane, and the starter said, "Runners take your mark." I got in my blocks. The starter said, "Set." I rose up, and then it happened: I left the blocks before the gun went off. I made a false start. If I did this once more, I would be disqualified. (This was back before the rule was changed. Today, if a runner has a false start, it is assigned to all the runners in that heat, and the next runner to have a false start is disqualified. Back when I was running, everyone could get one false start, and would be disqualified on the second one.)

There I was. I had made a false start in the 440. It was embarrassing. I got in the blocks, and all I could think was, "Do not do it again." My nerves got the best of me, and I made a false start for a second time. I had to walk off the track and face my teammates and my coach. When I saw my coach, he just shook his head and walked away, but his words from earlier in the week came back to me: "How you practice is how you will play." I hold onto the truth of that lesson to this day.

In 2002 Allen Iverson was playing basketball for the Philadelphia 76ers. He was at a press conference when one of the reporters questioned the efforts he was putting in at practice. Iverson got upset and said, "We're sitting here, and I am supposed to be the franchise player, and we're talking about practice...How silly is that?...We're talking about practice." He went on to use the word "practice" twelve more times in his rant. Iverson was downplaying the important of practice by pointing out how well he played. Iverson was a very good player, but his dismissal of practice is how most people will remember him. How you practice is how you will play.

When John baptized Jesus in the Jordan River, Jesus heard God say, "You are my Son, the Beloved; with you I am well pleased" (Luke 3:22). Afterward, Jesus made his way into the wilderness, where he fasted for forty days and forty nights. He was hungry, and then the first temptation came: "If you are the Son of God, command this stone to become a loaf of bread." Jesus resisted. He was then offered all the kingdoms of this world if he would turn away from God and worship the tempter. Again Jesus resisted. Jesus was then tempted to jump off the top of the temple: "If you are the Son of God, throw yourself down from here." For the third time, Jesus resisted. Luke ends this story of the temptation with these words: "When the devil had finished every test, he departed from him until an opportune time" (Luke 4:1–13).

For me, the temptations that Jesus faced in the wilderness all had a common thread: How was he going to accomplish what God was calling him to do? How was he going to live out his public ministry? Was he going to do it with amazing miracles? Would he take shortcuts, believing that the "ends justified the means"? Would he remain faithful to God? He "practiced" his responses to questions like that while he was all alone in the wilderness. It was that time of practice that prepared him for the other times, the opportune times, when the same temptations would return.

Peter, Jesus's disciple, tempted Jesus when Peter tried to convince Jesus that he did not have to suffer on the cross. Jesus responded by saying, "Get behind me, Satan" (Matthew 16:23). Jesus was fully aware of the source of Peter's objection.

Jesus was again tempted while he was on the cross. Some of the people in the crowd shouted out, "If you are the Son of God, come down from the cross" (Matthew 27:40). These were words that echoed out of the wilderness.

The temptation of Jesus is the background for the novel by Nikos Kazantzakis, *The Last Temptation of Christ*. In the novel, Jesus hears the tempting words, "If you are the Son of God, come down from the cross." He then dreams of living a life in which he did not suffer. He gets married and has children and grandchildren. When he finally awakens, he looks over and sees the nails in his hands, and he says, "It is finished." He resisted his last temptation. Jesus played the way he had practiced.

As Christians we are encouraged to participate in spiritual disciplines or spiritual practices. There is a twofold purpose for these practices: One, they help us to grow in our relationship with God. Two, they prepare us for our times of trial and temptation. For me, both purposes are important. It is important to connect with God in the present moment—to not think about where I have to go or what I have to do. It is important to sit still and to know that God is God, and I am not. It was Blaise Pascal who said, "All of humanity's problems stem from man's inability to sit quietly in a room alone."

If we are unable to sit in a room alone, we will never come to "know thyself." And without that self-knowledge and self-awareness, we will be vulnerable to every temptation that comes our way. Our spiritual practices prepare us for the game of life. Jesus once told a parable about a man who built his house on the rock and another man who built his house on sand. The house built on the rock was able to withstand the rains and the floods, while the house built on sand did not. (See Matthew 7:24–27.) Our spiritual practices prepare us for the rains and the floods that are sure to come. Jesus said that God "makes his sun rise on the evil and the good, and sends rain on the righteous and unrighteous" (Matthew 5:45). All of us can expect good times and bad times. That is life. And it is our spiritual practices, or lack thereof, that will greatly determine how we will respond. "How you practice is how you will play."

In one of my churches, there was a man named Charlie. He was a professional athlete and person of spiritual depth. He prayed, he studied, he served, and he lived out his faith in an uncommon way. When I would comment on his faithfulness, he would smile and tell me that he was "playing for an audience of one." It was clear that audience was God. Then tragedy struck: his wife died of cancer, and he was left with a young son. Charlie was brokenhearted. He grieved deeply, but he did "not grieve as others who have no hope" (1 Thessalonians 4:13). As I walked with him through this time, I was continually amazed at the strength of his faith. It was clear that his years of practice had helped to prepare him for that moment. "How you practice is how you will play."

There are a wide variety of spiritual practices, and there are two excellent books that will help you as you try to incorporate them into your life. They are *The Spirit of the Disciplines*, by Dallas Willard, and *Celebration of Discipline*, by Richard Foster. I encourage you to read one of them in order to learn more about the ways you can connect with God and prepare for your life in Christ. I would like to add that you should focus most of your practice on the things with which you most resonate. For example, if you are a highly extroverted person, you probably should not spend most of your time in silence or solitude. Or, as an introvert, you probably will not want to share your deepest needs in a group setting. If you are not a morning person, you do not have to get up before the sun to pray to the Son. I believe that the best spiritual practices for you are the ones that come the most naturally and easily to you, because those are the ones that you will consistently use. If you spend most of your time, especially in the beginning, focusing on the practices that are hard for you, you will give up.

This does not mean that you should never explore those spiritual practices that are difficult and challenging for you. Those are the things that you can do when you become comfortable with the disciplines you are already doing, and you need to be stretched. However, your basic practices should connect with who you are because they will best enable you to connect with God and prepare you for the temptations and the trials that are sure to come. "How you practice is how you will play."

For most of my life, I have struggled with anger and controlling my temper. When my children were young, I decided that, for their sake, I needed to do a better job of managing my anger. I knew that it was not something that I could do on my own; I had been trying for years. So I prayed about it. As I prayed I felt led to practice the discipline of meditation. I did not know much about it, so I read several books about Zen meditation. I gleaned ideas and practices from my readings, and I began to meditate. It was a turning point in my life—so much so, that if my children could sense that I was about to lose it, they would say, "Zen, Dad." The practice of meditation helped to change how I lived. Do not be afraid to learn from other traditions as you develop your spiritual practices.

Matthew Fox has written a book entitled *One River, Many Wells*. The basic message of the book is that there is a deep river of truth that flows from God and flows throughout the universe, and there are many wells that access that truth. Many of those wells are the spiritual practices that we make use of to connect with God. And it is those practices that fill us up and prepare us for the temptations and the trials that are sure to come. "How you practice is how you will play."

Hafez, a Muslim mystic (Sufi) from the 1300s, understood this connection between practice and play, as you can hear echoed in these words:

There is only one rule on this wild Playground,
every sign Hafez has ever seen reads the same.
They all say: "Have fun my dear, my dear, have fun,
in the Beloved's divine game,
O in the Beloved's wonderful game." (Fox 2004, 262)

"How you practice is how you will play."

CHAPTER 9

Perception Is Not Reality; Reality Is Reality

§

EARLIER I MENTIONED THAT ONE of the problems with proverbs is that they are not always true. Watched pots do boil. However, even though proverbs are not always true, they do point to things we know to be true. The same can also be said about clichés—those overused statements that people use when they do not really know what else to say. For example, one cliché that we often hear from certain religious types and professional athletes is "everything happens for a reason." In my opinion, this is just not true. If this is true, how do you account for senseless tragedies? What I believe most people are trying to say with that cliché is that everything has a cause, and that is true. But far too many people take the dangerous, theological step and declare that God is the cause of everything that happens. For me that theological stance is not acceptable when children starve to death or innocent people die in a terrorist attack or a troubled man with a gun kills strangers in a movie theater. In such cases there is a cause, but it is not because of reason or God.

Another cliché that is not always true is "perception is reality." That unfortunate statement is attributed to Lee Atwater, who was a political consultant. In the world of politics, how you are perceived by the public is very important, but that does not make it reality. I had a friend in one of the churches I served who loved to tell me that perception is reality. He would usually tell me that when someone in the church was upset with something that I had either not said, or that they had misunderstood. Once when he was trying to help me deal with a time of conflict, he said, "You have to remember that perception is reality." I looked at him, shook my head, and said, "No it isn't. Reality is reality."

One of the greatest thinkers to ever live was the Greek philosopher Plato. Plato used the allegory of the cave to explain how we come to know what is real. In the analogy, Plato asked us to imagine that there are prisoners in a cave who are chained in such a way that they can only look straight ahead at a cave wall. Behind the prisoners is a huge fire, and in front of the fire is a walkway. As the prisoners sit staring at the cave wall, people carrying various objects walk back and forth on the walkway, thereby casting shadows on the cave wall. The prisoners assume that reality is what they see on the wall in front of them, because that is all they have ever seen. Plato then said that we are to imagine that one of the prisoners is set free from his chains and turns around to see the people on the walkway, the fire, and the world outside the cave. The prisoner then comes to realize that his perceptions are not reality. For Plato this release from the chains of limited perspective and perception is the goal of education and the basis for his epistemology.

In 1 Corinthians 13:11–12, we can hear echoes of Plato's epistemology in the words of the Apostle Paul: "When I was a child,

I spoke like a child, I thought like a child, I reasoned like a child; when I became an adult, I put an end to childish ways. For now we see through a mirror, dimly [*we see shadows on a cave wall*], but then we see face to face. Now I know only in part; then I will know fully, even as I have been fully known." (Italics are mine.) Paul is telling us that what we see and what we know as human beings is limited, but one day we will be set free from this limitation.

Later, in 2 Corinthians 5:16–17, Paul wrote, "From now on, therefore, we regard no one from a human point of view; even though we once knew Christ from a human point of view, we know him no longer in that way. So if anyone is in Christ, there is a new creation; everything old has passed away; see, everything has become new." Again, Paul is telling us that we are to move beyond our limited, human perceptions—our limited, human point of view—and we are to allow God to open our eyes to the reality that is around us.

I believe Jesus was also telling us that perception is not reality when he said this to the scribes and Pharisees: "Woe to you, scribes and Pharisees, hypocrites. For you are like whitewashed tombs, which on the outside look beautiful, but inside they are full of bones of the dead and of all kinds of filth. So you also on the outside look righteous to others, but inside you are full of hypocrisy and lawlessness" (Matthew 23:27–28). Jesus was telling us that our perceptions—what we see or hear or feel or think—do not always enable us to arrive at the truth.

One of the great challenges of leadership—within the church and outside the church—is helping people become free from the belief that their limited perception is reality. This is even more important in times when people come to believe that their subjective understanding is the final arbitrator of truth. "This is what I think…I believe…I understand; therefore, it is true." This is a problem, and it is dangerous because it allows truth to become individualistic and personal perception to become reality. Leaders have the responsibility to try to help people understand that there is more to the reality of their lives than their limited perception.

Early in my ministry, I was in my office on a Friday writing my sermon for Sunday. My part-time secretary was off, so I was alone, which led me to believe that I would have a morning without interruptions. I was about to finish my sermon when a homeless man found his way back to my office. He told me that he was hungry, and he needed a change of clothes. I did not have time to deal with him; I had a sermon to write. So I decided to get rid of him by taking him across the street to the thrift shop that our church ran. I figured I would pass him off to the ladies over there and get back to my sermon. I told him to come with me, and I quickly walked him across the street.

Just before we got to the thrift shop, the homeless man said, "I have walked along the roadways for quite a while, and I have discovered that even weeds have flowers." His words made me stop. This man, who I was treating like an interruption and as something less than human, was telling me something that I believe God wanted me to hear. This man might seem like a weed, an interruption to my well-ordered life, but he was a person of value. This homeless man helped to open my eyes, and I become a little bit more open to the truth around me. I am not sure if the homeless man had ever read *Winnie-the-Pooh*, but Eeyore made a similar statement when he said, "Weeds are flowers too, once you get to know them."

Leaders need to help people see the truth that lies beyond our limited perceptions and perspectives, and I believe that the primary way we are to do this is by speaking up and challenging the things that are said as a result of those limited perceptions. This is difficult to do because people generally guard their perceptions with intense feelings. You have probably had the experience of telling someone that they did not know the whole story or have all the facts, only to have them respond with a surprising level of anger.

Many of us also avoid challenging people's limited perspective out of a sense of honest humility. "I am a person with a limited perspective, so who am I to tell people that they do not really understand the whole issue?" This question is very important because I believe that if we are to help people accept that they are seeing reality from a limited perspective, we must do so from a place of humility. You need to acknowledge your own limitations, while at the same time offering your insights. One way to do this is to start with where you agree with others' perceptions and then try to help them move beyond their limitations. "Yes, those are shadows on the cave wall, but look at what is happening behind you." This is a skill that I have tried to develop, especially in teaching situations.

When someone asks an argumentative question or makes an off-the-wall comment, I first try to find that place of agreement—a place from which we can start a discussion. In 1 Peter 3:15, it says, "Always be prepared to give an answer to everyone who asks you to give the reason for the hope that you have. But do it with gentleness and respect..." (New International Version). We best enable people to move beyond their limited perceptions when we relate to them with gentleness and respect and not with harsh judgment. We are best able to do that from a place of humility.

Humility as a leader also allows you to be open to an expansion of your own limited perspective or to embrace a new perspective that you had never considered before. New ideas and new thoughts are often dismissed because they do not fit into our way of seeing the world. A humble leader is one who is open to learning and expanding understanding.

Another challenge you will experience when you help set people free from their limited perceptions is that they will want to return to them. In Plato's analogy of the cave, he said that people who lived in the darkness and are forced to see the light will often go back to the darkness because the light hurts their eyes. We often go back to the chains that held us captive because we cannot live in the new freedom. In Exodus 14 we are told that the Israelites are standing on the shore of the sea and they see Pharaoh and his army approaching from behind and they turn to Moses and say, "Was it because there were no graves in Egypt that you have taken us away to die in the wilderness? What have you done to us, bringing us out of Egypt? Is this not the very thing we told you in Egypt, 'Let us alone and let us serve the Egyptians'? For it would have been better for us to serve the Egyptians than to die in the wilderness" (Exodus 14:11–12). The Israelites were slaves in chains in Egypt, but they would rather return there than go forth into their new reality.

Later, in the book of Numbers, the Israelites complain because they are tired of the manna that God had been providing for them. They say, "If only we had meat to eat! We remember the fish we used to eat in Egypt for nothing, the cucumbers, the melons, the leeks, the onions, and the garlic; but now our strength is dried up, and there is nothing at all but this manna to look at" (Numbers 11:4–6). People often want to return to the past as the memories of the pain and the problems fade away. Many of us ignore the words of Ecclesiastes, "Do not say, 'Why were the former days better than these?' For it is not from wisdom that you ask this" (Ecclesiastes 7:10).

People in the church often want to retreat to the "good old days" rather than facing their current reality. In one of the churches I served, there was a Sunday-school class that at one time had well over one hundred people in attendance every week; however, the members in this class were people in their seventies and eighties. Over the years, people of that class started to pass away or move away so they could be closer to their children. Eventually the class had about twenty or thirty people in attendance, but members continued to act like they were the largest class in the church. They demanded to meet in the same large classroom they had had for years, even though we had other adult classes that were outgrowing smaller rooms. They also wanted to have the same level of influence and power they had had when they were the largest class in the church. They refused to accept the reality that their class was dying off, and no one could convince them otherwise. My inability to help them turn from the shadows of the past was one of my biggest failings at that church.

There is no simple one-two-three approach to help people see and live the reality around them. It generally requires an individualistic and situational approach, which means that it also requires a lot of patience. We often speak of the "patience of Job," but I think the greatest example of patience in the Bible is Moses. For forty years he tried to lead the people of Israel through the wilderness, and it seems like they complained the entire time. When they no longer had to worry about the Egyptians behind them, they became afraid of the giants in front of them. Fear is one of the main reasons many of us refuse to open our eyes to the reality around us. So, in order to help people accept reality, you have to help them deal with their fears—especially the fear of letting go of what is familiar and comfortable.

One of a leader's most difficult tasks is to convince people that the familiar is no longer as comfortable as it once was. People who are comfortable where they are will not voluntarily move. It was the American author Finley Peter Dunne who is said to have originated the quote "comfort the afflicted, and afflict the comfortable." Those are two of a leader's tasks. You have to make sure that hurting people are helped, but you also have to say and do things that make people uncomfortable, otherwise they will be content to stare at shadows on the cave wall. One of the ways to do that is to convince people that the milk and the honey of the land over there is better than the cucumbers and the melons where they are. How you do that requires patience, and it also requires that you have a vision for where you want people to go and what you want them to do. You will need to share your vision in such a way that it makes people uncomfortable with where they are. And that requires patience because it takes most people a while to become uncomfortable with the familiar.

There is a song by the Eagles, "Already Gone," that contains the line, "So often times it happens that we live our lives in chains, and we never even know we have the key." So many people live their lives chained to the belief that their perceptions of things—their way of seeing things—is the only way of seeing things. Their chains keep them staring at the shadows on the wall in front of them. So one of the most important tasks of a leader—whether it is self-leadership (the process of becoming self-aware) or the leadership of a big organization—is to help people see that there is a key that can unlock their chains and set them free to see the world in a new way. That key is Jesus, who Paul said can make everything new—even you and me. Jesus is the key because he continually calls us toward the truth. He wants us to discover the truth about God's love for each of us, and he wants us to discover the truth about ourselves. He wants us to discover the truth that will set us free.

CHAPTER 10

Reading Really Is Fundamental

§

WHEN I WAS IN THE ninth grade, I was kicked out of Sunday school for asking too many questions. The teacher gave me a choice: either quit asking questions or leave. I left. I wandered around the halls of the church for a while, hoping I would find some doughnuts. Eventually I ran into Rev. Dave. He asked me what I was doing, so I explained to him what had happened. He took me to his office, pointed to the bookshelves that covered the walls, and he said, "Instead of going to Sunday school, you can come in here each week and read whatever book you want." The following Sunday, I picked *The Humor of Christ*, by Elton Trueblood. The title made me think that it might be a book filled with jokes and cartoons. (All life is junior high.) Instead, it was a book that created within me a desire to read. "Reading really is fundamental."

I encourage people to develop a plan for reading; otherwise we typically get into a reading rut, and we do not read a wide variety of books. I believe that you should read books that relate to your profession or your current stage of life, but you should also read classic literature and books that enable you to think new thoughts. I also believe that you should just read for fun, because that sort of reading provides an escape from the pressures of life. I have grown the most in my understanding of my life and of the world around me through reading. Throughout my ministry journey, I have read a wide variety of literature. I have read books on theology, leadership, psychology, philosophy, and other books that were not all that educational, but very entertaining. I remain convinced that reading is an indispensable part of the pathway of growth.

All of the chapters of this book were greatly influenced and shaped by the books I have read. So I thought it might be helpful to share some of the books that played a role in shaping each chapter.

Edwin Friedman's book *Generation to Generation* is what opened my eyes to the fact that "it's never about what it's about." Friedman was a family therapist and a Jewish rabbi, and in his book he explained many of the principles of family systems therapy. He explained what it means to be self-differentiated and how to be a nonanxious presence. He also helped me to understand how a family will try to blame all its problems on one family member (the identified patient), but in reality that person is only the symptom-bearer for the deeper, underlying problems of the family. Then, as a rabbi, he took his insights from family systems therapy and demonstrated how those same components were a part of the congregational family.

The classic novel *The Lord of the Flies* was often in the back of my mind when I passed on my understanding that "all life is junior high." In William Golding's novel, he told the story of a group of English schoolboys who were stranded on a deserted island and how they behaved in a world without adults. Some of the boys established rules and tried to live by them, while others played, and others became more and more violent.

Many people see this novel as a metaphor of how we are all capable of good and decent behavior and, at the same time, are also capable of evil. For me, this book reminds us that there are times when we will behave in ways that are much more similar to junior high than we would like to admit.

In the chapter on "making bones," I quoted Martin Luther King Jr., who said, "If you haven't found something worth dying for, you aren't fit to be living." I believe that the truth of that statement is fleshed out in many of King's sermons in his book *Strength to Love*. His sermons give incredible insight into who he was as a person and the theology behind the civil-rights movement of the 1960s. As you read his powerful words, you come to see that he discovered that for which he was willing to die.

One of the novels that I read because I felt like I should was *Steppenwolf*, by Herman Hesse. The novel tells the story of Harry Heller, who is convinced that he is comprised of two natures: a man and a "wolf of the steppes." The novel explores how Haller does not feel a part of the human world because of his "wolfish" nature, but he also wants to hold onto his humanity. His story is about the journey of coming to "know thyself" and of understanding his place in the world.

One of the most incredible and challenging books I have read is *Fear and Trembling*, by Søren Kierkegaard. The book is Kierkegaard's attempt to understand God's call asking Abraham to sacrifice his son, Isaac. Time and time again, Kierkegaard said that he would never be able to understand Abraham's faith; he could only admire it. This book challenged me to look at my own faith and my willingness to respond to God's call upon my life.

One of the strangest things I have read was Franz Kafka's *Metamorphosis*, which is the tale of Gregor Samsa—a man who awoke one morning as a gigantic insect. Internally, Gregor is still the same as he was before his transformation. He cares for his family, and he is deeply upset that he cannot go to work and provide for them. Eventually, his entire family rejects him. On one level he is rejected because of his appearance; however, on a deeper level, he is rejected because of his inability to work and provide for his family. His family members are upset by how Gregor's change has forced them to change. I think it is a story that asks this question: are we valued for who we are or only for what we are able to do for people?

Aristotle's *Ethics* is one of the books that changed my life because it helped me to understand the "doctrine of the mean." For Aristotle, a virtuous or happy person is one who discovers how to do the right thing at the right time for the right reasons. Therefore, a courageous person is not one who runs into every burning building, but one who does so when it is necessary and reasonable. In other words, Aristotle would tell us that we should not swing at every pitch in order to be virtuous; instead, we should swing when the time is right.

The truth that "we play the way we practice" is one of the themes of John Irving's novel *A Prayer for Owen Meany*. In this novel we are introduced to childhood friends, John Wheelwright and Owen Meany. Owen is abnormally small with a highly un-usual voice, which is expressed in the text by Owen's dialogue being written in capital letters. One of the things that John and Owen love to do is practice "the shot." John lifts up tiny Owen, who then dunks the basketball. Their ongoing practice of "the shot" becomes the way that John and Owen respond in a time of great danger for the people around them. Owen is a hero because of the way he lived his life and how that prepared him for what he encountered.

The Picture of Dorian Gray, by Oscar Wilde, speaks to how our perceptions are not reality. In the novel, Dorian Gray has his portrait painted, and he loves how it makes him look. He is young and handsome. He then makes a wish that he will never age or have his good looks tarnished but that his picture would "bear the burden" of his sins. And that is what happens. The picture on the canvas ages and is defiled by Dorian's constant search for plea-sure, but he remains young and handsome. No one ever saw the real Dorian Gray. In the end, Dorian goes to look at his picture, which he kept locked away in a room of his house, and the picture becomes something like a mirror. He sees what he really looks like and what he has really become. When he comes to see that truth, he kills himself. When his body is discovered, the people see the picture of a young and handsome Dorian Gray, but on the floor in front of it is an old and horribly disfigured man. What was reality? The Dorian Gray they had seen in public or the pic-ture that was locked away in a room for no one to see?

The book *Divine Conspiracy*, by Dallas Willard, helped me to become clearer about what I believe and how those beliefs shape who I am. Willard makes the point that all our actions come from what we think and that our thoughts are shaped by our beliefs. This book also provides the best overview of Jesus's Sermon on the Mount I have ever read. Willard challenged how I thought about God and how I understood myself.

For me, the most fundamental part of life is relationships, and that is why I believe the Bible is fundamentally about relationships. It is about our relationship with God and how that relationship is to shape every area of our lives. I think that being created in the image of God is about being in a relationship with God and that Jesus came into this world to restore that image as he taught us how to love God with all our heart, mind, soul, and strength and how to love the people around us. So my understanding is that the Bible is the book about relationships, and that is what life really is—what it's all about.

The books I have mentioned are some of the books that are on my list of the one hundred books I want to read before I die. I developed this list as a way of planning my reading and avoiding the reading rut. I have included my reading list so that it might help you to come up with a list of your own. I really do believe that reading is fundamental to our growth as leaders and as human beings.

One Hundred Books to Read Before I Die

1. *The Bible*
2. *The Great Gatsby*—Fitzgerald
3. *Slaughterhouse Five*—Vonnegut
4. *1984*—Orwell
5. *The Republic*—Plato
6. *Brothers Karamazov*—Dostoevsky
7. *The Catcher in the Rye*—Salinger
8. *The Lion, the Witch and the Wardrobe*—Lewis
9. *For Whom the Bell Tolls*—Hemingway
10. *The Picture of Dorian Gray*—Wilde
11. *The Grapes of Wrath*—Steinbeck
12. *Brave New World*—Huxley
13. *The Critique of Pure Reason*—Kant
14. *The Call of the Wild*—London
15. *The Rise of Theodore Roosevelt*—Morris
16. *Hitchhiker's Guide to the Galaxy*—Adams
17. *The Trial*—Kafka
18. *The Iliad and The Odyssey*—Homer
19. *Catch-22*—Heller
20. *Walden*—Thoreau
21. *Lord of the Flies*—Golding
22. *The Master and Margarita*—Bulgakov
23. *Bluebeard*—Vonnegut
24. *The Complete Works of Sherlock Holmes*—Doyle
25. *The Metamorphosis*—Kafka
26. *Confessions*—Augustine
27. *Do Androids Dream of Electric Sheep?*—Dick

28. *Zorba the Greek*—Kazantzakis
29. *The Idiot*—Dostoevsky
30. *Lady Chatterley's Lover*—Lawrence
31. *The Canterbury Tales*—Chaucer
32. *The Heart of Darkness*—Conrad
33. *The Divine Conspiracy*—Willard
34. *The Count of Monte Cristo*—Dumas
35. *The Red Badge of Courage*—Crane
36. *All Quiet on the Western Front*—Remarq
37. *The Complete Poems of Emily Dickinson*—Dickinson
38. *The Sun Also Rises*—Hemingway
39. *The Quran*
40. *One Hundred Days of Solitude*—Garcia Marquez
41. *The Maltese Falcon*—Hammett
42. *The Long Goodbye*—Chandler
43. *To Kill a Mockingbird*—Lee
44. *The Old Man and the Sea*—Hemingway
45. *Pensees*—Pascal
46. *The Little Prince*—de Saint-Exupery
47. *Candide*—Voltaire
48. *Bhagavad Gita*
49. *The Interpretation of Dreams*—Freud
50. *Zen and the Art of Motorcycle Maintenance*—Pirsig
51. *City of God*—Augustine
52. *Strength to Love*—King
53. *The Sound and the Fury*—Faulkner
54. *Ulysses*—Joyce
55. *The Scarlet Letter*—Hawthorne
56. *Blood Meridian*—McCarthy

57. *Waiting for Godot*—Beckett
58. *Crime and Punishment*—Dostoevsky
59. *Steppenwolf*—Hesse
60. *A Good Man Is Hard to Find*—O'Connor
61. *The Road Less Traveled*—Peck
62. *Don Quixote*—Cervantes
63. *A Prayer for Owen Meany*—Irving
64. *The Divine Comedy*—Dante
65. *The Hobbit*—Tolkien
66. *Night*—Wiesel
67. *East of Eden*—Steinbeck
68. *Leviathan*—Hobbes
69. *The Road*—McCarthy
70. *The Adventures of Huckleberry Finn*—Twain
71. *Ethics*—Aristotle
72. *The Plague*—Camus
73. *Generation to Generation*—Friedman
74. *Tropic of Cancer*—Miller
75. *Les Misérables*—Hugo
76. *The Adventures of Tom Sawyer*—Twain
77. *Women in Love*—Lawrence
78. *Animal Farm*—Orwell
79. *Tarzan of the Apes*—Burroughs
80. *Beyond Good and Evil*—Nietzsche
81. *A Tale of Two Cities*—Dickens
82. *Moby Dick*—Melville
83. *Aesop's Fables*
84. *Frankenstein*—Shelly
85. *The Complete Works of Shakespeare*

86. *Madame Bovary*—Flaubert
87. *A Farewell to Arms*—Hemingway
88. *The Stranger*—Camus
89. *Robinson Crusoe*—Dafoe
90. *Fahrenheit 451*—Bradbury
91. *On the Road*—Kerouac
92. *Treasure Island*—Stevenson
93. *The Invisible Man*—Wells
94. *Foucault's Pendulum*—Eco
95. *Fear and Trembling*—Kierkegaard
96. *Paradise Lost*—Milton
97. *The Prince*—Machiavelli
98. *Man's Search for Meaning*—Frankl
99. *Alice in Wonderland*—Carroll
100. *The Gift of the Magi*—O. Henry

One of the most common questions I get when people see my list of books, which is just in random order, is "have you read all one hundred?" My typical response is to quote the movie *Monty Python and the Holy Grail*: "I'm not dead yet."

CHAPTER 11

You Are What You Believe

§

EVERYONE HAS PROBABLY HEARD THE statement "you are what you eat." However, no one is quite sure of its origin. Anthelme Brillat-Savarin, a French lawyer and expert on gourmet food, wrote, "Tell me what you eat, and I will tell you who you are." He also wrote, "A dessert without cheese is like a beautiful woman with only one eye." Ludwig Feuerbach, a German philosopher, wrote, "Man is what he eats." Then in 1923, Victor Lindlahr, a nutritionist, wrote, "Ninety percent of the diseases known to man are caused by cheap food stuffs. You are what you eat" (www.phrases.org.uk/meanings/you-are-what-you-eat.html). Regardless of who first came up with the statement, we recognize its truth. You are literally shaped by the food you eat. In my opinion, it is also true that we are shaped by what we believe. "You are what you believe."

Dallas Willard, author of *Divine Conspiracy*—one of the books that has had the biggest impact on my life—wrote, "When we bring people to believe differently, they really do become different. One of the greatest weaknesses in our teaching and leadership today is that we spend so much time trying to get people to do things good people are supposed to do, without changing what they really believe...we always live up to our beliefs—or down to them, as the case may be" (Willard 1998, 307). If you really want to change people's behavior, including your own, you need to begin by changing beliefs.

In Jesus's first sermon, he said the following:

> You have heard that it was said to those of ancient times, "You shall not murder"; and "whoever murders shall be liable to judgment." But I say to you that if you are angry with a brother or sister, you are liable to judgment... You have heard that it was said, "You shall not commit adultery." But I say to you that everyone who looks at a woman with lust has already committed adultery with her in his heart...You have heard that it was said, "An eye for an eye and a tooth for a tooth." But I say to you, do not resist an evildoer. But if someone strikes you on the right cheek, turn the other also...You have heard that it was said, "You shall love your neighbor and hate your enemy." But I say to you, love your enemies. (Matthew 5:21–22, 27–30, 38–39, 43–45)

In each of those statements, Jesus is taking his listeners' long-standing beliefs, and he is calling on them to change what they believe because he wants them to change their behavior.

Earlier I mentioned that for twelve years, I served on a denominational committee that had the responsibility of examining candidates for ministry. During those twelve years, I insisted on two things: Firstly, that the candidate had a certain degree of self-awareness. Secondly, I wanted the candidate to have a well-thought-out theology. As I have stated, it is self-awareness that enables you to better understand why you do the things you do. But on an even more important level, it is your beliefs that are the source of your attitudes, your assumptions, and your actions. What you believe matters because you always live up to it, or you will live down to it.

What you believe about God makes a difference in who you are and how you live. If you believe that God is harsh and judgmental, just watching for you to mess up so that he can punish you, those beliefs will have an impact on your life and relationships. With that sort of understanding of God, you will often become a timid person who is afraid to do anything enjoyable for fear that you might possibly do something wrong. Or you might go in an opposite direction and become like the God in whom you believe. In that case you will become harsh and judgmental, ready and willing to point out the sins of everyone else.

Stuart was a man in the church where I worked while I was in seminary, and he was obsessed with what he saw as other people's inaccurate beliefs and inappropriate behavior—especially mine. We continually clashed because we had very different understandings of God. I believe that God is a God of grace, and it is because of that grace that God understands our flaws and failings, and he is forgiving. Stuart's God was much more like the Calvinistic preacher Jonathan Edwards, who believed that God sees us like a spider dangling from a thin web above the flames of hell. And, like Edwards, Stuart's God was more than ready to drop us into flames for even the slightest infraction of the law. Stuart was harsh in his judgments. He was an angry man who people tried to avoid. And I believe that Stuart's lack of forgiveness came from his inability to accept God's forgiveness for himself.

I believe that was what Jesus was speaking about when he said, "For if you forgive others their trespasses, your heavenly Father will also forgive you; but if you do not forgive others, neither will your Father forgive your trespasses" (Matthew 6:14–15). I do not think that Jesus was saying that God's forgiveness is conditional or that our actions make God unable to forgive us. What I understand Jesus to be saying is that we will be unable to receive God's forgiveness, as a gift of grace, if we refuse to forgive others. It is our inability to forgive others and ourselves that becomes a barrier to the forgiveness that God is ready to pour into our lives.

Our lack of forgiveness is like a kink in a hose. The water is on, but it is the kink that keeps it from flowing. God's forgiveness is a gift of grace that is freely offered to all, but as long as you believe that your forgiveness is something that must be earned, then you will be unable to receive God's grace for yourself. And when you believe that forgiveness is something that must be earned, you will try to do whatever you can to earn it, and you will carry the burden of wondering if you have been good enough.

In the New Testament, the word for forgiveness literally means to let go of something. So the process of forgiving is letting go of the hurt and the anger that you have because of what someone else said or did. If we refuse to forgive, then we carry around that hurt and anger inside us. One of the things Mark, my backpacking friend, taught me is that the lighter your pack is, the easier the hike will be. You do not want to carry around stuff that you really do not need. Likewise, if you choose not to forgive those who have hurt you and made you angry, then you will be carrying around burdens that make your journey through life much more difficult.

One of the great offers Jesus made to us is this: "Come to me, all of you that are weary and are carrying heavy burdens, and I will give you rest" (Matthew 11:28). Jesus can give you rest from carrying around the heavy burden of hurt and anger, if you will allow him to teach you how to forgive and how to receive forgiveness. Father Richard Rohr writes, "If you have forgiven yourself for being imperfect and falling, you can now do it for just about anyone else. If you have *not* done it for yourself, I am afraid you will likely pass on your sadness, absurdity, judgment, and futility to others" (Rohr 2011, 114). You are what you believe.

What you believe about Jesus makes a difference in who you are and how you live. In his book *The Many Faces of Christology*, Tyron Inbody writes, "Not one of us in our Christology, no matter how fundamentalist, evangelical, creedal, liberal, scholarly, revolutionary, or cynical, will ever permit our image of Jesus to be anything more or less than we find necessary for salvation, whether salvation be pardon from sin, or reunion with God, or sanctification, existential decision, Gnostic enlightenment, or postmodern irony!" (Inbody 2002, 41.) Or more simply stated, your understanding of the meaning and purpose of life is shaped by what you believe about Jesus. If you believe that Jesus was just a good man, then you will understand that the goal of life is just to be a good person and that it is because of your goodness that you will be saved from hell. If you believe that Jesus was just a great teacher, then the goal of your life will be to acquire more and more knowledge, and you will believe that your knowledge will save you from whatever may lie ahead. If you downplay or deny the humanity of Jesus, you are a Docetist, and you will believe that the physical side of life is the source of sin and that salvation will be your release from your body and this evil world. Almost everyone has an opinion about Jesus, and those opinions—those beliefs—shape who you are, how you live, and your future hopes.

In my personal Christology, the most important thing I can say about Jesus is that he was God incarnate. The incarnation of God in the man Jesus means that Jesus was fully God and fully human. Jesus embodied God. Jesus showed us who God is. He lived out the love and grace of God as he proclaimed that our sins are forgiven. By doing this, he showed us how to become like God. This is not something we can do on our own, as we learn from the story in Genesis of the Fall. Instead, it is something that can only be given to us by the grace of God.

The Jewish leaders often got upset with Jesus when he said, "Your sins are forgiven." This upset them because they believed that only God was able to forgive sins. (See Matthew 9:2–8.) They could not see or accept that Jesus was God in their midst—in the flesh. Jesus showed us who God is.

Jesus also showed us what it means to be fully human. He showed us how we are to love one another. He showed us how we are to forgive those who hurt us and make us angry. He also showed us, by becoming a flesh-and-blood human being, that we are to value and enjoy the physical aspects of life. The created world, which God said was good, is still good. It is so good that Jesus came to live in it. Our physical bodies are a good creation of God, not a prison from which we need to escape. We are to find joy in this life.

One of my wife's greatest pleasures and joys is going to the beach. Many times she will go to the beach so that she can connect with God. For her, the ocean is a symbol of God. The ocean appears limitless. It is vast. It is full of life. It is constant, as one wave crashes on shore after another. Sitting in the sand and looking out at the ocean is a sacramental moment for her. A sacramental moment is when we allow the ordinary events of life to speak to us about God and his love for us, just as the ordinary elements of bread, wine, and water communicate to us the grace and love of God.

The incarnation of Jesus teaches us to value this life and to be open to God speaking to us through the most ordinary and common events of life. Elizabeth Barrett Browning wrote, "Earth's crammed with heaven, and every common bush afire with God, but only he who sees takes off his shoes; the rest sit round and pluck blackberries." What you believe shapes who you are and how you live. You are what you believe.

The incarnation of Jesus tells me that the goal of being a Christian is deciding how we will live in the here and now; it is not primarily about where we will go when we die. So often, Christians become fixated on going to heaven or avoiding hell, and in the process they shift the focus from beliefs to behavior. But as Dallas Willard made clear, beliefs are more important than behavior because your behavior flows out of what you believe. "You are what you believe."

How do your beliefs about God and Jesus shape your relationships? Good question. That is what we will explore in the next, and final, chapter.

CHAPTER 12

You Put Your Whole Self In

§

I FIRST STARTED VISITING KEY West, Florida, in 1974, when I moved from North Dakota to Florida, and now I live in this incredible place. Key West is surrounded by water and filled with all sorts of interesting people. The city has also been the home to many talented people, including Jimmy Buffett. One of Jimmy Buffett's lesser-known songs is "What If the Hokey Pokey Is All It Really Is About?" The chorus of the song goes like this:

> Maybe it's all too simple
> for our brains to figure out.
> What if the Hokey Pokey
> Is all it really is about?

What is this life really all about? I believe the answer to that sort of fundamental question can only be answered by going back to our origin—back to why we were created. In the first chapter of Genesis, we read one version of the creation story. Toward the end of that story, God said, "'Let us make human-kind in our image, according to our likeness; and let them have dominion over the fish of the sea, and over the birds of the air, and over the cattle, and over the wild animals of the earth, and over every creeping thing that creeps upon the earth.' So God created humankind in his image, in the image of God he created them; male and female he created them" (Genesis 1:26–27).

We were created to bear the image of God. That is what life is about, but now we have to figure out what that means. Almost no one believes that the image of God has to do with our physical appearance. Most understand it to mean something more important, something deeper. Some say the image of God is our capacity to reason or our capacity to create life or that it is our conscience. I believe the clue to figuring out this concept is the word "us." When God was preparing to create people, he said, "Let us create humankind…" Elsewhere in the first chapter, God simply spoke and it happened. Some dismiss this use of the word "us," saying that it is God using the "royal we." They point out the similarity in the second surah of the Quran where God repeatedly speaks as a "we." I think there is more to it.

I believe we are created by a God who is an *us*. As a Christian, I understand that *us* to be the Trinity. We are created by a God who—at his very essence, at the very core of God's being—is in an eternal relationship. Therefore, to be created in the image of God means that we are created for relationship. We are created to be in relationship with God, with other people, and with creation. I first began to understand the image of God in this way when I read Jurgen Moltmann's book *God in Creation*. In that book he writes, "The *imago Dei* is neither the indestructible substance of the human being, nor can it be destroyed by human sin. We have defined it as God's relationship to human beings" (Moltmann 1985, 232).

What is life really about? In one word...relationships. We are created by God to be in relationship with God, one another, and creation. We are created to put our whole self into our relationship with God and the people who are a part of our lives.

In the second story of creation, recorded in Genesis 2–4, we hear about what is commonly called *the Fall*. The idea of the Fall is that it attempts to tell us why we are not the people God created us to be. The story tells us that the punishment for our disobedience to God is that we will be separated from God when we are thrown out of the garden. We will be separated from one another, as the man and the woman were no longer equals, but the "husband shall rule over you." There is now a separation in humanity. And we are separated from creation through futility and fear. Futility entered into the good creation because the ground was cursed, and the man would have to labor in order to get anything to grow. And fear entered into the good creation with the serpent's punishment. The story of the Fall is the story of how we became separated from God and his intended purpose for our lives.

Jesus comes to us as God in the flesh to forgive our sins, which is something only God can do. And he comes to recreate us in the image of God—again something only God can do, because only God can create. Jesus comes to teach us and show us and enable us to be in relationship with God and with one another. He said that all the Law and the Prophets can be summed up in this way: "You shall love the Lord your God with all your heart, and with all your soul, and with all your mind. This is the greatest and first commandment. And the second is like it: You shall love your neighbor as yourself" (Matthew 22:37–39). "You put your whole self in."

We were created to be in relationship with God and with others, and Jesus makes it clear that we do that through love. In other words, we were created to love God, to love one another, and to love the created world. Love is the key to really understanding what this life is all about. And to really love someone, you put your whole self in.

John Wesley, the founder of the Methodist movement, in his sermon, Original Sin, said, "You know that the great end of religion is, to renew our hearts in the image of God." Wesley believed that the goal of religion—its great end—is to restore our relationship with God, one another, and creation. If you believe this, then it will have an impact on all of your relationships, especially your primary ones.

As I tried to make clear in the previous chapter, forgiveness is essential for our relationships with both God and with others. It is through God's forgiveness of us that the separation between us is overcome, and we are invited back into a relationship with God. If we are unable to acknowledge our need for forgiveness, we will most likely not believe that we need to be in relationship with God.

Forgiveness is also essential in our interpersonal relationships. It is essential because if we spend an extended time with another human being, it is inevitable that we will do something to make the other person angry, or we will say something that hurts him or her. It is a certainty that we will need to be forgiven. The reverse is also true. People we love and care about will hurt us and make us angry, and we will have to decide whether we will forgive them or not.

As we focus on forgiveness, it is important to understand that there is a difference between forgiveness and reconciliation. I believe that you must forgive those who have hurt you and have made you angry, but you do not always need to reconcile. Forgiveness is a one-way street. The decision to forgive is something you can do all by yourself. You choose to let go of your anger and hurt.

Reconciliation is a two-way street that you do not always have to travel. There are some offenses so great that you should not stay in a relationship with a person. The abusive parent needs to be forgiven, but that does not mean that you have to be in a reconciled relationship with him or her. You also cannot reconcile if the other person does not want to do his or her part in repairing and restoring the relationship. In those cases, you choose to forgive, and you move on.

Understanding this difference between forgiveness and reconciliation has been helpful when I have met with people who were still carrying around a load of hurt and anger toward a deceased parent. When I served in Sebastian, Florida, I was often asked to conduct funerals for people who did not have a church. Since I did not usually know the person who had passed away or his or her family, I would meet with the family so that I could get some idea of who the person was and could deliver an appropriate eulogy. I will always remember the time I sat down with two sisters, Ann and Kathy. Their mother had just passed away, and I was meeting with them to plan the funeral. I asked them to tell me about their mother, and Ann looked at me and said, "We are just glad the mean old bitch is dead." My first thought was, "Well this will be a tough eulogy to write." But my next thought was about the hurt and anger these two young women must have been feeling. I asked them to tell me more about their mother, and they shared with me their pain and anger from years of verbal and emotional abuse. They told me how nothing they ever did was good enough for their mother. After a while, I shared with them my belief that they would need to forgive their mother if they were to move on through their grief and find some sense of peace. They felt like they were unable to forgive her because they could no longer communicate with her. They argued that since their mother could not ask for their forgiveness and that they could not tell her that they have forgiven her, their forgiveness would not make any difference. I explained to them that forgiveness is a one-way street. You choose to let go of the hurt and the anger, or you choose to continue to carry the burden. Forgiveness is a decision you make because you know that God has forgiven you. And even though they would never be able to reconcile with their mother, they could forgive her and they would no longer have to carry around their anger and hurt.

Another thing I believe is essential for a healthy relationship is mutuality. There needs to be a sense of give-and-take and shared sacrifice if the relationship is to be a lasting one. I was once in a relationship when the other person said, "We are friends because you always do what I want." That is not the foundation for a healthy relationship.

In Mark 8:22–26, there is an interesting story about Jesus healing a blind man. After Jesus laid his hands on the blind man, he asked him if he could see. The blind man said, "I can see people, but they look like trees, walking." Jesus then laid his hands on the man again, and his sight was fully restored. We can take away a couple of things from that story. First, healing is often a process. We may not be healed of the hurt and the anger from the deep wounds of the past immediately. It may take a while before we are at the point that we can forgive and move on. The other thing we can learn is that we are not the people we were created to be if we see the people around us like trees. Think about what you do with a tree. You use a tree. You make stuff out of its wood. You cut it down when it is in the way. When you see people in the same way that you see a tree, you will use them, and that is not how we are called to love one another.

The reality is that all people will have relationships that are one-sided, where one person does all the giving, and the other does all the taking. And there are often some very practical reasons for why we may want to maintain those relationships. For example, there will be times when you will have to care for a person who is totally dependent on you, like a newborn baby or a dying parent, or you may put up with that sort of a relationship because you have an overly demanding boss and you want to keep your job. But those relationships will be draining and will seldom be long term. Mutual relationships are the ones that fill us up and keep us going.

I was going through a very difficult and demanding season of ministry, and one evening I told Terri that I felt like one of those old-fashioned pumps with a handle that you have to move up and down to get water. I said, "It seems like everyone in the church is just pumping me for what they want, and I have nothing left to give." She listened, she cared, and she understood, and in that moment that was all I needed. Over the following few days, I remembered that it was my relationship with her and with God that were the ones that could fill me up so that I could continue to deal with the needs of the church. We all need relationships that fill us up, and the ones that do that the best are ones built on mutuality.

I want to mention one other thing about mutuality, especially the aspect of mutuality between a husband and a wife. Many in the church maintain that the Bible teaches that men are to rule over women, particularly when it comes to marriage. As I read the Bible, I discovered that setup was the result of the Fall. It was not what God intended. The husband ruling over the wife was punishment for sin. (See Genesis 3:16.) But those who are Christians, who are having the image of God restored in us, can return to the equality that God intended, as we affirm the words of the Apostle Paul who said, "There is no longer Jew or Greek, there is no longer slave or free, there is no longer male or female; for all of you are one in Christ Jesus" (Galatians 3:28). God's will for our relationships is mutuality, because that is how we love our neighbors as we love ourselves.

Another essential element for a healthy relationship is patience, especially if you have come to see that all life is junior high. We have to be patient with one another's childish and selfish behavior. And we need to appreciate when others are patient with ours.

In his book *Falling Upward*, Father Richard Rohr makes a very interesting observation. He writes, "Some theorists say you cannot stretch more than one step above your own level of consciousness, and that is on a good day! Because of this limitation, those at deeper (or 'higher') level beyond you invariably appear wrong, sinful, heretical, dangerous, or even worthy of elimination" (Rohr 2011, 10).

One of the reasons that we need to be patient with one another is that we are all at different levels of development—mentally, psychologically, and spiritually. As you first think about this, you might be tempted toward arrogance and think that you are smarter or more spiritual than someone else, but remember, "Arrogance and self-awareness seldom go hand and hand." However, the awareness that we are all at different levels of development is not arrogance; it is reality. And if we want to nurture those relationships, we will have to be patient with one anther.

As I look back on my ministry, I can now see that I was often frustrated with people in the church because they did not understand some of my leadership decisions or my theological stance. Sometimes I was wrong, and it was a good thing they did not go along with me. However, there were other times when I knew I was right, and I just had to be more patient as I waited for them to grow in their understanding. I had to learn to be more forgiving of criticism that, at times, came out of a lack of understanding on their parts. In one of my appointments, a very conservative woman was convinced that I was not a Christian because I did not believe some of the things she believed. She had a very literal and limited understanding of the Bible. I did not. But I was patient with her. I pushed when necessary; I waited when needed. On my last Sunday at that church, she hugged me and said, "I have learned more from you than you will ever know."

We are all at different levels of development, so if we are to be in relationship with one another, we will need to be patient with one another.

In *Divine Conspiracy*, Dallas Willard wrote, "Intimacy is the mingling of souls who are taking each other into themselves to ever increasing depths" (Willard 1998, 163). I believe we all crave relationships like that—relationships where we have deep and growing connections with others. It is the development and maintenance of those relationships that make life worth living, because that is what life is really all about. Maybe Jimmy Buffett was onto something because, at the end of the hokey pokey, you put your whole self in. The most meaningful and fulfilling relationships are the ones where you put your whole self in, and that includes your relationship with God.

BIBLIOGRAPHY

Fox, Matthew. *One River, Many Wells.* New York: Penguin, 2000.

Friedman, Edwin H. *Generation to Generation.* New York: Guilford Press, 1985.

Heath, Chip, and Dan Heath. *Made to Stick.* New York: Random House, 2007.

Inbody, Tyron. *The Faith of the Christian Church.* Grand Rapids: Eerdmans, 2005.

Inbody, Tyron. *The Many Faces of Christology.* Nashville: Abingdon Press, 2002.

Lewis, C. S. *The Four Loves.* New York: Harcourt and Brace, 1960.

Moltmann, Jurgen. *God in Creation.* San Francisco: Harper & Row, 1985.

Plato. *The Great Dialogues of Plato.* New York: New American Library, 1956.

Rohr, Richard. *Falling Upward.* San Francisco: Jossey-Bass, 2011.

Thoreau, Henry David. *Walden.* New York: New American Library, 1960.

Willard, Dallas. *The Divine Conspiracy.* San Francisco: Harper, 1998.

John B. Hill graduated with a BA from Florida Southern College and master's of divinity from Emory University. He has served in small and large United Methodist churches since 1981. His wide range of experience over those thirty-four years inspired him to write Lessons Learned along the Way to help others who work in churches or relate to people on a regular basis.

He is married to Terri, and together they have three children and six grandchildren.

If you would like to contact John you can do so at jbhill4455@gmail.com and you can follow his blog at johnhillinkeywest@wordpress.com.

Made in the USA
Charleston, SC
21 February 2017